AN EARLY TOLL-ROAD
The Dublin–Dunleer Turnpike, 1731-1855

Maynooth Studies in Local History

GENERAL EDITOR Raymond Gillespie

This pamphlet is one of five new additions to the Maynooth Studies in Local History series in 1996 and adds to an ever growing literature of local history in Ireland. The studies are all drawn from theses submitted as part of the Maynooth M.A. course in local history which began in 1992. Each essay is an exploration not of particular places, usually identified by administrative boundaries, but rather of how in the 'little places' of Ireland their inhabitants lived out their day-to-day lives in the past. As a result the range of subjects covered in these essays is as broad as the experience of any one or even a group of individuals.

Many things bound people together, and drove them apart, in the past and pressures for change came from both within and without regional societies. These bonds and divisions are reflected in these studies: religion at parish level, the comonalities of living in the same town, parish or landed estate, or places where they met each other, such as schools, or fought with each other, as at fairs. It is these complex realities which give the Irish historical experience its richness and diversity and which can only be fully appreciated at the local level and from a series of chronological and geographical perspectives.

These Maynooth Studies in Local History, like the earlier volumes in the series, help us to build more complex pictures of the reality of the Irish past from the middle ages to the present and in doing so presents local history as the vibrant and challenging discipline that it is.

IN THIS SERIES

Maynooth Studies in Local History: Number 5

An Early Toll-Road

The Dublin–Dunleer Turnpike, 1731-1855

David Broderick

IRISH ACADEMIC PRESS

Set in 10 on 12 point Bembo by
Verbatim Typesetting & Design, Dublin
and published by
IRISH ACADEMIC PRESS LTD
Kill Lane, Blackrock, Co. Dublin, Ireland
and in North America by
IRISH ACADEMIC PRESS LTD
c/o ISBS, 5804 NE Hassalo Street, Portland, OR 97213

A catalogue record for this title
is available from the British Library.

ISBN 0-7165-2595-X

Printed in Ireland
by Colour Books, Dublin

Contents

Preface

I wish to acknowledge with gratitude some of the many people who helped in the completion of this study.

I am indebted to Ms Tina Hynes, archivist Fingal County Council; to the library staff of St Patrick's College Maynooth, Trinity College Dublin and the National Library; to Mr J. Walsh, librarian, Balbriggan and Mr G. Morgan of Man-of-War; to the Director of the Ordnance Survey and to Mr P. Hughes and above all to Dr J. Hill and Dr R. Gillespie of St Patrick's College Modern History Department.

I also wish to thank my wife and family for their support and patience.

Introduction

Even God cannot change the past.

Agathon (quoted in Aristotle's *Nicomachaean Ethics 6*)

This study will trace the history and development of a portion of the principal road (modern N1) from Dublin to Belfast during its period of time as a turnpike road from 1731 to 1855. The portion of the road concerned extends from Dublin city via Drumcondra and Santry (now northern suburbs of Dublin city) to Swords and from there northwards via Balbriggan and Drogheda to the village of Dunleer in county Louth. The location of this road is shown on the general location map (Map 1). The distance from Dublin to Dunleer is approximately thirty-eight miles or thirty Irish miles.

It is remarkable that very little research has been done on turnpike roads in Ireland and no complete history of any such road has ever been published. This may be due to the scarcity of records. Many of the Irish turnpike road records were kept in the Public Records Office[1] in the Four Courts in Dublin. This record office was destroyed in 1922 in the course of the Irish civil war. Some records not in the Four Courts did survive, but these are incomplete and, in some cases, fragmentary.

The only two published papers on individual turnpike roads in Ireland are E. O'Leary's 'Turnpike roads of Kildare, Queen's county, etc. in the eighteenth century'[2] and J.J. Leckey's 'The end of the road: the Kilcullen turnpike 1844-1848 compared with 1787-1792'.[3] O'Leary's article, which was published in 1914, gives details from portions of the records then in the Public Record Office concerning two roads: one from Naas in county Kildare via Maryborough to Ballyroan in Queen's county (now county Laois), and the other from Mountrath in Queen's county via Frankford (Kilcormac) to Clonefin in King's county (now county Offaly). The paper is short but of value. J. Leckey's article is a well researched and interesting one which essentially compares two different periods of the Dublin to Kilcullen turnpike road as shown in the relevant minute books.

Apart from these articles, there are references to turnpike roads as parts of other books, papers and a thesis.[4] These books include those with references to turnpike roads in England such as *The story of the king's highway*[5] by Sidney and Beatrice Webb. The history of other forms of transport in Ireland, for example, canals, navigation and railways is fairly comprehensively covered but turnpike roads appear to have been neglected.

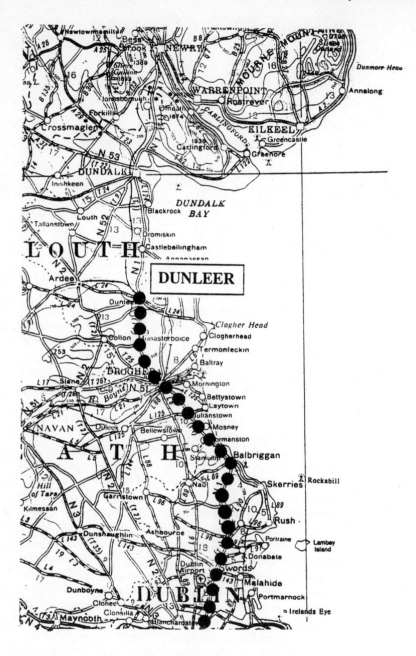

Map 1 General location map
Scale: 1 inch represents 9 miles. Based on the Ordnance Survey by
permission of the Government. Permit No. 6169.

The aim of this study is, therefore, to fill a void in Irish local history and to show how the Dublin–Dunleer turnpike road came into existence, how it operated and how it ended. The study deals with three distinct themes: legislation and finance, travellers and traffic, influences and engineering and this has entailed the use of a variety of sources. Included among these sources are the surviving manuscript records of the trustees of this turnpile road, relevant legislative and parliamentary records and contemporary maps and accounts.

The surviving manuscript records of the Dublin–Dunleer turnpike trust date from 1775 to 1855 and are held at Fingal County Archives. Though these records are probably the most extensive of any Irish turnpike trust, they are non-continuous and fragmentary. It is difficult, with a source such as this, to know how representative the surviving material is of the total material. However, the advantage of using such material is that it was written either at, or very close to the time when the events happened. The council's archivist has divided these records into a preliminary shelf, box, and file list which will be used when references are made to any of these records.

The legislative and parliamentary records consist of the revelant statutes, the Irish house of commons journals[6] and parliamentary registers of the eighteenth century[7] and the parliamentary papers of the nineteenth century. The house of commons journals are useful for providing the parliamentary reports drawn up at the request of parliament on either single turnpike roads or groups of them. The journals cover the full period of the Irish house of commons but the parliamentary registers only cover the period from 1781 to 1800. These registers recorded the parliamentary debates, so it is possible to ascertain the views of the parliamentary members on various bills before the house. The parliamentary papers are the proceedings of commissions or committees of inquiry set up to investigate particular problems. These bodies published not alone reports of the findings of the inquiries but also the evidence both written and oral submitted to the inquiries. This evidence is often of more interest and value to the historian than the reports themselves, as they give information on the views of the ordinary interested citizens about problems.

It is fortunate that the area in which the Dublin–Dunleer turnpike road was situated was covered by a number of maps over the years. The maps found most useful were those from 1762 onwards on which the locations of the turnpike gates were marked. Other contemporary sources such as newspapers and travellers' accounts need to be handled with care and should be cross-checked where feasible. This is because of the possibility that what one observer considered a very good road another observer at the same time may have regarded as a very poor one. Sources such as these accounts and pamphlets or tracts putting forward certain viewpoints have to be assessed with the general intention of the writer in mind.

The ultimate source for any road history is site evidence. Portions of the Dublin–Dunleer turnpike road still exist and only the carriageway surfacing has been altered. Some of the bridges are still in existence and there are also a number of milestones (using Irish miles) on the road which helped to locate proposed improvements referred to in the legislation.

Lastly it must be pointed out that it was necessary to use a number of technical and archaic terms in this book. These are explained in the appendix.

Origin, Legislation and Finance

The eastern coast of Ireland, north of Dublin, consists of gently rolling lands interspersed with rivers flowing eastwards to the Irish Sea. The two major rivers are the Liffey, which flows into Dublin bay and the Boyne which flows into the Irish Sea about twenty-six miles further north. Many invaders and settlers sailed up these rivers. The first to arrive were the Neolithic people about 3500 BC. The Celts came about 400 BC and in the fifth century, Christianity was brought to Ireland and soon religious establishments and monasteries were set up at suitable locations along the coast. Between the ninth and twelfth centuries, Norse, Norman and English invaders and settlers arrived. These founded and later built up and fortified the towns of Dublin on the Liffey and Drogheda on the Boyne. The settlements and monasteries required land communication as well as communication by sea. So bridges and lengths of road were built to facilitate these north-south and south-north movements until eventually one road was formed extending from Dublin via Drogheda and Dundalk to the Ulster area. The first traveller to describe a portion of this route was Bishop Chericati, papal nuncio at the court of King Henry VIII and a friend of Erasmus, who wrote in 1515[1]

> ... leaving Dublin, we passed over level ground pleasing to the eye, overlooking the sea, until we came to Drogheda a fairly rich territory, five miles distant from the sea.

It is difficult to say which route the bishop followed, as only in a short section from Balbriggan to Gormanston would the sea be visible to anyone following a reasonably direct route.

By 1647, the exact location of this northern road from Dublin is known. In the first Irish road book *A guide for strangers in the kingdom of Ireland*, published in London that year,[2] part of the road to Londonderry from Dublin via Dundalk is described as being:

Dublin to Swords – six miles
Swords to Balrudderie – six miles
Balruddery (sic) to Drogheda – eight miles
Drogheda to Dunleare – eight miles
Dunleare to Dundalk – ten miles

The 'miles' used were Irish miles but the distances were far from accurate.

In 1690 the Boyne area near Drogheda became the major battleground between King William of Orange and the Catholic King James II. It is fortunate that a first hand account of travel on the road from Dublin to Drogheda in May 1690 has survived in the journal of Captain John Stevens who fought in the army of King James II at this battle. The following extracts are from this journal and describe the portion of the road from Swords to Drogheda[3]:

> Tuesday ye 20th about 5 of the clock in the morning I returned to the Regiment and found them ready to march. It was ordered that neither Officer nor souldier (sic) should quit the ranks, which was no small fatigue the weather being hot and the road excessive dusty, to that degree that we were also stifled and blinded, and so covered with dust that we scarce knew ourselves, all which fell most grevously upon such as marched afoot, whereof I was one. From Swords to Bellagh is 4 miles, thence to Ballruddre 2 both of them poor villages, these last 2 miles of the longest I have seen. Hence to Gormanstown 3 miles, not worthy the name of a town, but at best only a tolerable village, most remarkable for giving title to a Ld., who has a good house in the place, but poorly provided at that time, as some of our Officers found by experience, who went to it only to get any sort of drink, there being then none to be had for mony (sic). Here we made a halt for about 2 hours, but found no refreshment, but what we brought with us unless the coole air and grass. Hence we marched 2 miles farther to Innistown bridge, where we drew up in a large feild (sic) in order to pitch our tents but before the ground was marked out orders came to march to Drogheda, three miles from this place, and we were quartered in the City, where we found one Battalion of His Maties foot guards, the Earle of Tyrones Regiment of foot and 100 of his Guards. All the country between this citie and Dublin is very pleasant, and a good soile, having great store of corn some good pasture, the road in summer very good, but in winter extreme deep unless helped by an old broken causeway full of holes.

Describing the town of Drogheda, Capt. Stevens wrote:

> On this side also is the mound not so large as capable of being made strong, and has the full command of the whole city. Both parts are joyned by a wooden Bridge, as high as which close to the keys ships of considerable burden have water enough, but the river though deep is narrow.

Another traveller in 1708 was Dr Thomas Molyneux, who travelled from Dublin to Drogheda and Dundalk via Santry, Swords, Bellough and Julianstown. Dr Molyneux who left Dublin in August, 1708[4] '... came in three hours and half to Bellough, a small village, thro' a very flat open corn country, good cawsey roads, passing thro' Santry, and Swords which last is a Burrough'. In 1714, Moll's Map[5] of that year shows the general location of the road based on the latest survey of Henry Pratt. It should also be noted that in 1722, the wooden bridge at Drogheda was replaced by a stone structure.[6] In 1728, a map[7] of the counties of Ireland was published which showed the main roads including the Dublin to Dunleer one, three years before its conversion to a turnpike road.

The early roads of Ireland prior to 1600 were, with notable exceptions, natural tracks on which stone and/or gravel was placed from time to time. These tracks, or roads, were probably maintained by the local sept or clan on an irregular basis. At that time, in the rural parts of Ireland except for a small area around Dublin city and county and parts of counties Kildare, Meath and Louth called the Pale, Irish rather than English rule prevailed. However almost all the towns were in the hands of the Normans and English who built strongholds at various strategic locations throughout the county.

By the early seventeenth century, the English authorities began to assert their influence more widely and in 1613 the parliament in Dublin passed the first act dealing with road maintenance. This was entitled 'an act for repairing of highways and cashes'[8] and was based on a similar act[9] in England of 1555 and as later amended. Under this act, the parish, under the aegis of the grand juries, was made the unit responsible for the maintenance of all public roads, and all landowners, cottiers and labourers were obliged to give six days free labour each year to repair and maintain the roads in the parish.

Grand juries were to play a major role in Irish road administration down to 1898 and so it is best to set out exactly how these bodies were formed. The following description is taken from *Roads in Ireland* by P.J. Meghen.[10]

Under the feudal system the Norman knights were given estates on the conquered lands and in return, they were to give services to the king in times of war. They were also bound to pay the king certain dues. A king's officer was appointed in each shire or county to collect these monies and to call on the armies when needed. The division of the county into shires or counties was a slow process and was not completed until 1610. The sheriff was to make a visit to his county twice each year and he also summoned the feudal tenants to meet the king's visiting judges twice a year at the county town. From this gathering, he selected twenty-three of the chief landowners and this body was known as the grand jury. From the evidence that survives, it appears that this body as well as advising the judges on law cases also dealt with financial matters and questions of general information. This was the body entrusted with the care of roads and bridges.

In the case of bridges an act[11] was passed by parliament in Dublin in 1634 which stipulated that bridges, causeways and toghers in the highway were to be repaired or built by the inhabitants of the county or borough in which they were situated or in the case of intercounty bridges, each county was to contribute its share. The act gave the grand juries powers to levy a county cess or tax to fund these works.

Because of the Cromwellian and Williamite wars very little progress was made with road and bridge improvements throughout the seventeenth century. However after 1690, the county settled down and agricultural and industrial output started to increase, thus creating the need for a better system of communication and roads. This increased trade is shown by the attached table taken from a table in L.M. Cullen's *An economic history of Ireland since 1660*[12] giving Irish exports and imports from 1700 to the fifth day of January 1816.

Table 1 Exports and Imports of Ireland from 1700 to 5 January 1816

Year ending 25 March	Exports £	Imports £
1700*	814,746	792,473
1720	1,038,382	891,678
1740	1,259,853	849,678
1760	2,139,388	1,647,592
1780	3,012,179	2,127,579
5 Jan 1801	3,714,779	5,584,599
5 Jan 1816	7,076,123	6,106,878

Meanwhile the poor condition of the roads and indeed of the vehicles was becoming more apparent. John Brown, writing in 1729,[13] stated:

> Our whole inland carriage at present performed by small feeble cattle either in high loads, which scarcely exceed two hundred weight; or on truckle carts, of which a horse and car in summer-

* Year ending 25 December

time, when the roads are dry and the cattle strong may, one with another carry about four hundred weight; but in other seasons of the year there is little or no land carriage; for those little machines are swallowed up in bad roads ...

In 1729 also, Dean Swift,[14] who had travelled extensively stated: 'Generally speaking all over the kingdom, the roads are deplorable.'

Meanwhile, the deficiencies of the six-day labour system were becoming apparent. Dublin at this time was growing rapidly and its population had increased from approximately 9,000 in 1666 to about 90,000 in 1730. The city was being rebuilt on a grand scale with a linen hall built in 1728 and the new parliament building begun in 1729. All the main routes into Dublin from all over Ireland came in through county Dublin. The grand jury of that county found that the six-day labour system, which was only intended to repair local parish roads could not cater for heavily trafficked through-routes and they made their case to parliament in 1719[15] and again in 1729.[16]

The difficulty such as that of the grand jury of Dublin county in maintaining heavily trafficked through-routes had already become apparent in England much earlier. The solution adopted there was to oblige the through-traffic to contribute towards the cost of the road repairs. This was first done in 1663 under an act[17] relating to a section of the great north road. This contribution was collected at a toll-gate or turnpike set up at the entry to the section of the road concerned, by a trust set up for that purpose. Though not a great success early on, the idea of the turnpike road administered by a trust spread rapidly in England in the last decade of the seventeenth century and early decades of the eighteenth. Trusts were empowered to raise loans by means of debentures backed by the tolls collected and then could use the available funds to repay the loans, meet their expenses and improve the roads. The parliament saw turnpike roads as a way of getting improved roads at no expense to public funds.

A good description of why turnpike roads were originally introduced is given in the *Report of the commissioner on propriety of maintaining or abolishing turnpike roads in Ireland* of 1856:[18]

> When smooth and level roads between distant points were required for the safety and ease of passengers and the rapid transmission of intelligence, and when the conveyance of merchandise began to be a matter of great importance, it did seem hard that small communities should be charged with providing expensive facilities for others; the value of which they themselves but little understood.

In 1729 the Irish parliament passed an act[19] which made the road from Dublin to Kilcullen in county Kildare the first Irish turnpike road. On 8 October 1731 an order in the Irish house of commons stated:[20]

> That leave be given to bring in the heads of a bill for repairing the road leading from the city of Dublin to the town of Drogheda and that Mr Hill and Captain Whitshed do prepare and bring in same.

On 19 October 1731[21] Mr Hill, according to order, presented to the house:

> the heads of a bill for repairing the road leading from the city of Dublin to the town of Dunleer in the county of Louth, which were received and read and committed to a committee of the whole house on Thursday next.

It is not known why Mr Hill and Captain Whitshed decided to extend the proposed turnpike road from Dublin to Drogheda by a further eight miles to Dunleer. It is possible that this was done at the instigation of Francis North or Thomas Tenison, the members for the corporation of Dunleer, or through the influence of the Foster family from the Dunleer area. Thus in 1731 the Dublin–Dunleer Road together with a number of others were made into turnpike roads under their own acts. As the eighteenth century progressed, various other routes mainly in the south and west of the country were converted into turnpike roads. Similarly a number of other routes in the north of the country were also converted including the one from Belfast southwards towards Dundalk and from Dundalk to Dunleer by an act of 1774.[22] New turnpike roads were still being created in the nineteenth century though by then there were far fewer being initiated.

The portion of the Dublin to Belfast road between Dublin and Dunleer in county Louth became a turnpike road in March 1732 by an act[23] of the Irish parliament. This act set up a turnpike trust to operate the road and named 237 individuals as trustees. All these were holders of high office in the state or established church, titled persons or large landowners along the route. The act empowered these trustees to erect turnpike gates and toll houses and to collect the specified tolls from the different types of traffic using the road; for example for every coach, berlin, chariot, calash, chaise or chair drawn by six or more horses the sum of one shilling and so on down to a rate of one half-penny for every horse, mare, gelding, mule or ass, laden or unladen, and not drawing (see Table 2 for details of toll rates under this act).

The act gave powers to the trustees to use the toll-funds collected to pay for the expenses of procuring the act, the cost of erecting the toll

Table 2 Toll rates, as in 1731 act (5 Geo. II, c.15)

Traffic Unit		Toll rate per unit
1 Coach, berlin, chariot, calash, chaise or chair	drawn by six horses or more	1s. 0d.
2 Coach, berlin, chariot, calash, chaise or chair	drawn by 2 to 5 horses	0s. 6d.
3 Waggon, wain, cart or carriage with 4 wheels,		1s. 0d.
4 Waggon, wain, cart or carriage with 2 wheels	drawn by more than one horse, mare, gelding, ass or mule	0s. 3d.
5 Carriage (chair) or chaise	drawn by one horse, mare or gelding	0s. 3d.
6 Car or other carriage	drawn by one horse, mare or gelding	0s. 1d.
7 Horse, mare, gelding, mule or ass laden or unladen, and not drawing		0s. 0.5d.
8 Drove of oxen or neat cattle	unit rate per score and proportionately for a greater or lesser number	0s. 10d.
9 Drove of calves, hogs, sheep or lambs	unit rate per score and proportionally for a greater or lesser number	0s. 5d.

houses and toll-gates and for road repairs. In addition, this act empowered the trustees to borrow such sums as were required to improve and repair the road by way of debentures raised on the security of the tolls. It also required that repayment of principal and interest on these debentures was to be funded out of toll receipts. This act, which was intended to last only for twenty-one years, had a large number of provisions about the operation of the turnpike road.

It should be noted that under this act, the entire length of the turnpike road, that is, the thirty Irish miles from Dublin to Dunleer, was made the responsibility of the trustees only, and the act did not oblige the grand juries to provide funds or 'six-day labour' or any portion of it to the road. This was different from the system of turnpike roads which generally prevailed in England at that time and also differed from the legislation for the Dublin-Kilcullen turnpike road previously mentioned. The parish six-day labour system of road maintenance prevailed in England from 1555 to 1835 and most turnpike road trusts in that country were either allocated a share of this free labour in their enabling acts or were given an unspecified share which they had to negotiate with the relevant grand juries. In Ireland, the six-day labour system was never popular, nor did it ever work satisfactorily. This may be because it was administered and managed at local level by parish appointees who often did not even speak the language of the indigenous population. The system was abandoned in Ireland between 1759 and 1765 and replaced by a local taxation system.

The 1731 act was quickly brought into operation. It appears that the condition of the road was far worse than was originally thought. As a result of a report to the Irish house of commons in November 1733 which showed that the trustees had already borrowed £11,000 to meet expenses to date, a new act[24] was passed in 1733. This new act made provision for the repayment of this £11,000 by raising the tolls and extending the life of the 1731 act until 1773. The tolls were increased by factors of from fifty to one hundred per cent. This act also made provision to enable the trustees to borrow a further £3,000 and repay both it, and the yearly interest due, from the toll-receipts. Lastly, the act stipulated the methods of issuing debentures and payment of same and optimistically provided that if the sums borrowed were paid off and the road was then satisfactory before 1773 both this act and the 1731 act should cease to apply.

Thus, it can be seen that from the outset this turnpike road went into serious debt and that the gravity of this was neither realised by the trustees nor the legislators. It is difficult to state the exact debt at this stage. However the evidence given by Arthur Barlow, treasurer of the Dublin–Dunleer trust, to the Dublin turnpike inquiry 1854,[25] indicated that all the money was borrowed under the 1731 act; the whole of the debentures or at least all he had seen, bore the date 1735 and the original capital raised was 270 shares at £50 each, that is, £13,500.

It is obvious that Mr Barlow had a lapse of memory when he made this statement as the only debenture that has survived is debenture number 193 which was dated September 1734,[26] and Mr Barlow paid the interest on it in November 1840. This debenture was made out to Alderman Richard Grattan and interest on it was paid intermittently over the years up to July 1846.

The Dublin–Dunleer turnpike road was not alone amongst the Irish turnpike roads in having financial difficulties at this time. It soon became obvious by the middle of the eighteenth century that most of the turnpike roads in Ireland were unable to pay their debts. Dr Cooper read a report to the Irish house of commons in February 1758[27] based on the results of an inquiry carried out by a committee headed by him into the financial position of the turnpike roads.

This report showed the following position (note monetary sums are rounded off to the nearest pound in the interest of clarity):

1 There were twenty nine turnpike road trusts which together owed £133,290 in debentures.
2 Interest on the debentures of eighteen of these turnpike trusts was at six per cent per annum and on two others was at five and one half per cent per annum and on the debenture of nine others including the Dublin-Dunleer road trust was at five per cent per annum.
3 The yearly interest on the debenture of all twenty-nine road trusts was £7,576 giving an overall indebtedness on debentures, amounts of interest and compound interest equal to £169,827.
4 The total length of turnpike roads involved was 627.25 Irish miles (average length 22.4 Irish miles) and the total operating cost was £4,645.
5 The total yield was £11,197 and so the net income over expenditure was £6,552.

The committee was of the opinion that instead of £133,290 only £88,629 needed to have been borrowed and that the unnecessary debentures raised should be clawed back. They also found that there was mismanagement of the tolls and recommended that all debentures be reduced to five per cent per annum, that the produce of the tolls of all the turnpike roads be paid into one aggregate fund with the turnpike trusts classified into three categories based on dates of establishment of the trusts and that a scale of priorities to be introduced for the payment of creditors according to these classes. It should be noted that the Dublin-Dunleer road was named in the first category, that is, it merited the earliest payment.

This report was one of the best and most comprehensive on turnpike finances. It is sad that the report was not implemented and expanded so as to create a national turnpike road system under which the tolls collected throughout the country would be allocated on the basis of need.

From the above report it is known how the turnpike roads were functioning from an official point of view, but this was at variance with the views of the public. In 1763 there was a leading article in the *Freeman's Journal*,[28] which gives some insight into how the turnpike roads were viewed at this time. In this article the writer stated

There is no instance in which the complaints of the public are better founded than those universally made of the ruinous and almost impassable condition, in which the highways of this kingdom are found; nor are there any taxes so severe as those on passengers on the turnpike roads of the whole kingdom, even to the gates of our metropolis; where the traveller at this day cannot be said to receive value for the excessive tolls, payable on all parts of these roads, while they are universally found in a worse condition than they have been known within the memory of man before turnpikes were instituted.

A report on the Dublin–Dunleer and Dundalk–Banbridge turnpike roads was presented to the house of commons in February 1764.[29] This showed that the average amount of money available for road repairs over the previous seven years on the Dublin–Dunleer road was £303 1s. 0d. The report also made recommendations, most of which were incorporated into a new act which, though dated 1763,[30] did not come into effect until May 1764. This act increased the tolls and made them payable once per day between Dublin and Gormanston bridge and once per day between Gormanston bridge and Dunleer. It also stipulated that portions of the road were to be realigned and that drivers of vehicles with wheels narrower then three inches should pay one shilling at every toll gate.

The act resulted in an increased income from the tolls but still the available funds for road repairs were stated to be inadequate in a report[31] dated November 1767 on the Dublin–Dunleer and three other turnpike roads. The report also indicated that the payment of interest to the Dublin-Dunleer debenture holders was overdue for two and a half years. No reason was given as to why the interest on the debentures had not been paid. Even though the amount available for road repairs had more than doubled, much more money must have been needed since the report added that there were two reasons why the road was in bad repair: the want of proper gravel pits, and the expense of breaking stones. It is not easy however to see why these two problems should have brought about such a sudden change and it can only be concluded that there must have been poor management not to have spread the available funds more evenly over a longer period.

In 1773/4 yet another act[32] was passed which directed that, since the section of re-alignment west of the existing road, as specified in the 1763 act, had not been carried out because of cost, the trustees should now attempt a shorter realignment east of the modern road. By 1787, the financial state and physical condition of the turnpike road was again a cause of concern. In February 1787[33] a report was submitted to the Irish house of commons. The main findings of this report indicated that the sum of £13,500 in debentures was still due together with the annual interest of £675 and the toll income was £1,350 which after deduction of the annual interest and salaries, left only £592 14s. 6d. for road repairs. In addition, the report stated that the condition of the road had deteriorated badly and the sum available for repairs was totally inadequate. The report made a number of other recommendations, most of which were accommodated in a new act[34] passed that year. This major new act repealed all previous acts and changed the controlling system. The act divided the road into three divisions: southern division (Dublin to Lissenhall bridge, which is about one mile north of Swords); middle division (Lissenhall bridge to the eighteenth milestone at Gormanston) and northern division from the eighteenth milestone to the bridge of Dunleer.

The act nominated a large number of leading persons as commissioners to take full charge of the trust and the road and under these commissioners it nominated seven trustees for each of the above divisions. It should be noted that one of the trustees of the middle division was Maurice Leonard of the Man-of-War. Man-of-War was the name of a roadside inn situated about three miles south of Balbriggan. New toll rates were also specified in this act (see Table 3 for details) and tolls were only to be paid once per day in the same division.

The toll rates in this act were however made more rational in that the increases were kept to a minimum and the prices for the common carts or cars were reduced. These toll rates held for forty-two years until 1829 and it is probable that they influenced the type of traffic which used the road during that period, that is, they favoured the small cars, carts and cart-cars drawn by the single horse (see analysis of traffic in 1818 in the next chapter).

It should be said at this stage that the official answer from 1733 onwards to rising debt was always to increase the tolls. It seems that it never occurred to the legislators to reduce the tolls to encourage greater usage of the road and so increase the total toll-take. Though there is no way of ascertaining the elasticity of demand for travel on this road in the eighteenth century, it is most probable that many travellers took slightly longer routes to avoid paying tolls at all. This is obvious from the increasing expenditure of the grand juries on the non-turnpike roads. The reduction of tolls in the 1787 act must be balanced against the fact that drivers who travelled the full length of the road now had to pay tolls three times in a single journey.

Two further acts were passed in 1788[35] and 1789,[36] the former again changing the management system of the road and the second making provision for the re-alignment of the road so as to by-pass the steep hill near the Man-of-War inn. These acts did not change the toll rates. The 1789 act provided for raising a loan of up to £10,000 by debentures at six per cent per annum to finance the by-pass of the Man-of-War hill but, perhaps wisely, no action was taken on raising this loan. The 1789 act also

Table 3 Toll rates, as in 1787 act (27 Geo. III, c.59)

Traffic Unit		Toll rate per unit
1 Coach, landau, chariot, chaise, phaeton, cabriolet, curricle or chair,	drawn by six or more animals	2s. 8½d.
2 Coach, landau, chariot, chaise, phaeton, cabriolet, curricle or chair,	drawn by four or five animals	1s. 7½d.
3 Coach, landau, chariot, chaise, phaeton, cabriolet, curricle or chair,	drawn by two or three animals	1s. 1d.
4 Coach, landau, chariot, chaise, phaeton, cabriolet, curricle or chair,	drawn by only one animal	0s. 6½d.
5 Waggon, wain, dray, cart, car, timber, or other carriages not included in 1,2,3 or 4 above	price per animal drawing, when wheels are four or more inches wide and smooth★	0s. 1d.
6 Waggon, wain, dray, cart, car, timber, or other carriages not included in 1,2,3 or 4 above	price per animal drawing, when wheels are between three and four inches wide and smooth	0s. 1½d.
7 Waggon, wain, dray, cart, car, timber, or other carriages not included in 1,2,3 or 4 above,	price per animal drawing, when wheels are less than three inches wide and smooth	0s. 3d.
8 Waggon, wain, dray, cart, car, timber, or other carriages not included in 1,2,3 or 4 above,	price per animal drawing, when wheels are not smooth	1s. 0d.
9 Horse, mare, gelding, ass or mule, laden or unladen,		0s. 1d.
10 Oxen, cows, neat cattle,	price for score and proportionally for greater or lesser numbers	1s. 8d.
11 Calves, sheep, lambs or pigs,	price for score and proportionally for greater or lesser numbers	0s. 10d.
12 Cars with smooth wheels of any width, where the axle tree is fixed, that is, it does not rotate with the wheels	per animal drawing	0s. 1d.

★ See term four in appendix.

provided that Mr Maurice Leonard, the owner of the Man-of-War inn, be awarded £1,000 compensation for loss of business should the by-pass be carried out.

At this time trade was increasing and the finances of this turnpike were given an added boost by the introduction of mail coaches in the 1790s. The post office paid over a fixed sum every quarter to the turnpike trustees for the use of the road by their coaches. It is noted from the records of the turnpike road[37] that in the year ending on 5 April 1808 a total of £532 7s. 0d. was paid by the post office, and similar sums were paid in other years. Indeed the period from 1790 to 1819 was the most productive in toll-receipts for the whole period of existence of the turnpike roads in general including the Dublin–Dunleer road.

The figures for total toll receipts for the period 1812 to 1828 for the Dublin–Dunleer turnpike road shown below are derived from the evidence submitted to the select committee on turnpike roads in Ireland[38] set up in 1831. They show the reduction in receipts after 1819 together with the main reason for this, as submitted by the trustees (see note below).

Table 4 Toll-receipts on the Dublin-Dunleer turnpike road
from 1812 to 1828

Year	Receipts £ s. d.
1812	4,426
1813	4,190 10s. 0d.
1814	4,269 10s. 0d.
1815	4,410 10s. 0d.
1816	4,740
1817	4,312 18s. 7d.
1818	3,986 15s. 1d.
1819	4,156 10s. 0d.
1820	2,912 11s. 1d.
1821	2,994 14s. 8d.
1822	2,945 8s. 9d.
1823	2,376 5s. 10d.
1824	2,324 4s. 1½d.
1825	2,067 12s. 9½d.
1826	1,789 10s. 7d.
1827	1,949 7s. 3d.
1828	1,914 14s. 0d.

Note: The decrease of tolls since 1819 had been chiefly caused by the opening of the road from Dublin to Drogheda via Ashbourne.

These figures show that the income was falling, and in 1829, a new act[39] was passed by the United Kingdom parliament which raised the tolls. Some of the tolls were raised by fifty to one hundred per cent above their previous levels. (see Table 5 for details).

Table 5 Toll rates, as in 1829 Act (10 Geo. IV, c.63)

Toll rate per horse or other beast drawing of the eight listed groups of vehicles	*Toll rate per animal drawing*
1 Coach, berlin, landau, vis-à-vis, chariot, chaise, phaeton, cabriolet, calash chair, caravan, hearse or litter	6*d.*
2 Gig, jaunting car or dog cart	4.5*d.*
3 Waggon, wain, cart, dray, carriage (excl. car) with streaks or shoeings of all wheels, six inches or more wide and with no projecting nails, bolts, or screws	2*d.*
4 Waggon, wain, cart, dray, carriage (excl. car) with streaks or shoeings of all wheels between three and six inches or more wide with no projecting nails, bolts or screws	4*d.*
5 Waggon, wain, cart, dray, carriage (excl. car) with streaks or shoeings of all wheels, less than three inches wide and with no projecting nails, bolts or screws	6*d.*
6 Cars with streaks or shoeings on all wheels less than four inches and more than two and a half inches wide with no projecting nails, bolts or screws	2*d.*
7 Car with streaks or shoeings on all wheels less than two and a half inches wide with no projection nails, or screws	6*d.*

8	Cart or car having any streaks or shoeings of any wheel where there are projecting nails, bolts or screws		6*d*.
9	Horse, mule, ass laden or unladen		1½*d*.
10	Drove of oxen, cows or neat cattle	unit rate is per score and pro rata for greater or lesser numbers	6*d*.
11	Drove of hogs, calves, sheep or lambs	unit rate is per score and pro rata for greater or lesser numbers	10*d*.
12	Mill stones	Rate per mill stone	0*d*.
13	Carriage not drawn by animals	Rate same as similar carriage drawn by two animals	

This act resulted in an immediate short-term increase in income for the trust as shown by table 6 using figures taken from the trustees' evidence to the select committee on turnpike roads in Ireland 1831-32.[40]

Table 6 Toll receipts on Dublin-Dunleer turnpike road from 1828-31

Year ending 24th Jan	Income
1828	£1,914. 14*s*. 0*d*.
1829	£2,293. 18*s*. 2*d*.
1830	£2,789. 18*s*. 1*d*.
1831	£2,572. 1*s*. 0*d*.

The financial state of the Dublin–Dunleer turnpike trust as submitted to this select committee of inquiry in 1831-2 showed that the principal outstanding was still £13,500 (Irish currency) or £12,461 10*s*. 9½*d*. (British currency) and arrears of interest due was £3,401 10*s*. 9½*d*. (British currency). It is thus seen that even through the years of high income, neither the principal nor the interest was reduced.

The road and trust were now heading for even worse financial times following the end of the wartime boom in agricultural prices after 1815. Throughout the rural part of Ireland poverty was becoming widespread, culminating in the Famine in 1845 in which it is estimated that approximately one million people died of starvation or disease. However the biggest effect on the road finances was brought about by the opening of the Dublin-Drogheda railway line in 1844 which reduced the road toll-receipts considerably and so increased the debt due. By the year 1854 the financial position of the Dublin-Dunleer trust and road was critical, for example the capital owed was £12,461 11s. 4d. sterling[41] (£13,500 Irish) together with £9,163 0s. 4d. sterling in arrears of interest. In 1855 an act[42] was passed by the U.K. parliament which ended the term of the road as a turnpike. Under that act debenture holders only received ten per cent of the nominal value of their holding. The road itself reverted to the control of the respective grand juries, that is, those of county Dublin, county Meath, Drogheda and county Louth.

It is remarkable that the only capital debt incurred on this road, was raised within three years of the start. As stated, the greater part of this money was used to erect gates and gate-lodges and to effect major repairs to the road at that time. Over the greater part of the next 121 years of this road's operation, the trustees managed to pay as much of the interest on this capital debt as possible and to maintain the road. However in the later years of the existence of this turnpike road, toll-receipts fell so much that the arrears of interest increased until they amounted to approximately seventy five per cent of the outstanding capital sum. The condition of the road deteriorated accordingly.

There seems to be little doubt but that if parliament had paid off this capital debt and outstanding interest at any time, the toll-receipts would have been sufficient to maintain this road to a very much higher standard and so probably attract more traffic and consequent tolls. It is ironic that the Irish parliament were so frugal with public money in respect of turnpike roads, in view of the very large sums spent by them in subsidising the building of canals and river navigations. It is difficult to see why this should have been so. Obviously the Irish parliament like the British parliament in the eighteenth century assumed that the road system was merely of local importance and that traffic could always manage to 'muddle through' despite the poor condition of some roads. The French government on the other hand realised the economic advantages of a good national road network very early in the eighteenth century and so constructed good arterial roads.

Travellers and Traffic

The first direct knowledge of the traffic on the Dublin–Dunleer road comes from *The Gentleman's and Citizen's Almanack* compiled by Samuel Watson[1] for each year, commencing in 1733. The 1733 *Almanack* described the road as a principal one and indicated the post towns and the frequency of such post. The 1738 *Almanack* gave details of the first stage-coach service on the road:

> The Drogheda stage-coach set up at the Boot Inn, Drumcondra Lane, sets out from Dublin at 8 in the morning in the winter quarter on Tuesdays and Saturdays and comes to Dublin on Mondays and Fridays.

As the years went by, these services increased in number and frequency and the journey times decreased. To cater for this new traffic new inns were opened or existing ones refurbished along the turnpike road. A notice in the *Dublin Journal*[2] stated

> On or after 25 February 1746 the Drogheda Landau which was run between Dublin and Drogheda through Santry and Swords on

Figure 1 Painting of Man-of-War inn by John Nixon, *c.*1790
(in private ownership)

Mondays, Wednesdays and Fridays, returning the following days and dining at the *White Hart* near Balrody [Balrothery] will run on Tuesdays, Thursdays and Saturdays from the *York Minster* in Capel Street and dine at the Man-of-War now kept by Mrs Jane Wilson.

This oddly named Man-of-War inn which is located about three miles south of Balbriggan was in existence before the turnpike road as a notice in another newspaper *The Dublin Intelligence* in 1722[3] indicated

Thomas Carson wigg-marker [sic] at the Hen and Chicken in Caple [sic] Street, now keeps the Man-of-War between Dublin and Drogheda; where there is good entertainment for man and horse.

Since this inn became the stopping place for breakfast for travellers leaving Dublin and travelling northwards, it became famous and was and will be forever associated with the Dublin–Dunleer turnpike road. Visitors to the inn who recorded the fact in their diaries and note books included: Mary Delaney in 1752,[4] the artist Gabriel Beranger in 1781,[5] the Irish patriot Theobald Wolfe Tone in 1792[6] and Dr John Gamble in 1810.[7] Dr Gamble has left a good description of breakfast at this inn:

The bread and butter, tea, sugar and cream were excellent ... In this country 1s. 7.½d. is the regular charge for breakfast and includes everything, eggs, ham, etc. The latter however is not generally called for, eggs being the favourite dish of the country, as well as potatoes. I eat one, some ladies eat one also; the gentlemen however took care none should be last; some eat four and one eat six with a proportional quantity of bread and butter.

Travellers continued to come to this inn until 1834 when a major road realignment scheme resulted in the by-passing of the Man-of-War hill. An entry in the *Leigh's new pocket road book of Ireland*[8] (1835 ed.) stated:

Man-of-War was formerly a first stage from town and well known for its excellent accommodation, but it has fallen into decay in consequence of the high road being changed.

In order to visualise how travel on an early turnpike road such as this appeared, the note-book of one early visitor named John Loveday[9] who travelled on the newly created Dublin–Kilcullen turnpike road in 1732 is of interest. In that note-book he wrote:

This was a very fine made way of considerable breadth … but just out of Dublin are cottages made of mud, there was a calf to each cabbin; great numbers of poor along the road. Even in Dublin the poorer boys go without shoes and stockings, and as we came into the country men, women all sort, either had none or carried them on their shoulders if they were travelling the road.

In another section of the book he remarked on the traffic.[10]

They have no carts or waggons here, they have carrs, which are a kind of sledges, set on two solid wooden wheels, straked with iron and drawn by a single horse; they carry great burthens, some 600 weight.

The traffic in the eighteenth century seemed to consist of the large carriages of the wealthy classes, the stage coaches for those who paid to be conveyed for one place to another and the carts or cars drawn by a single horse where were used for conveying merchandise. The stage coaches were becoming more numerous and venturing further afield. From Constantia Maxwell[11] it is learned that

On August 13th 1752, the first stage coach set out from Dublin to Belfast. It was drawn by six horses and took three days for the journey; but the enterprise was not a success perhaps on account of the roads, and it was not until 1788 that a regular service was instituted.

One of the most distinguished visitors was Arthur Young[12] who came to Ireland in 1776, and travelled extensively throughout the country. He visited Balbriggan in July 1776.[13] He wrote at length on the roads and traffic in the country, but was not an admirer of the turnpike roads, though he praised the non-turnpike ones, for example he stated[14]

For a country, so far behind us as Ireland to have suddenly got so much the start of us in the article of roads, is a spectacle that cannot fail to strike the English traveller exceedingly. But from this commendation the turnpikes in general must be excluded; they are as bad as the by-roads are admirable. It is a common complaint that the tolls of the turnpike are so many jobs and the roads left in a state that disgrace the kingdom.

and added, after again praising the by-roads 'In a few years there will not be a piece of bad road, except turnpikes in all Ireland.'[15]

This writer also commented on the traffic using the roads and considered that their relatively good condition was due to the fact that 'nearly all
goods transported by road are carried in small loads (between six and ten
hundredweight) by one-horse cars or carts and not by the large English-
type wagons which were so destructive of the roads there'.[16] He concluded
that, because of this, the unit cost of transporting goods in such a manner
must have been up to five times the cost of the transport of similar goods
in England.[17]

It is of interest to note an advertisement in a Dublin newspaper of
1768 which, whether well intended or not, foreshadowed the changes
which would one day drastically alter the world's roads and road traffic.
The advertisement announced a demonstration of a new Phaeton-mobile
or flying chariot[18] and stated:

> The phaeton will travel on the road without horses or cattle, six or
> eight miles an hour; it will ascend a hill with ease and descend no
> faster than the rider pleases; it is five hundred weight and set in
> motion and stopt [sic] with a finger.

This may have been some early form of steam-driven vehicle, as the
steam engine had been invented in 1710 by Thomas Newcomen. James
Watt invented the condensing steam engine in 1765, though he did not
patent it until 1769. However no more was heard of the Phaeton-mobile
in Dublin. This is not surprising as it was almost thirty-five years later
before the first crude steam traction engine or locomotive went into service. The first mention of a steam coach in Dublin was in February 1820
when an advertisement for one operating from Dublin to Belfast on the
turnpike roads was inserted in the newspapers.[19] It should also be mentioned that in the 1829 act[20] for the Dublin–Dunleer turnpike road, a provision was made in the new toll rates for charging for vehicles not drawn
by animals (see Table 5). However the steam-driven vehicle was never
really the great success its advocates expected and it was not until the
internal combustion engine came, long after the turnpike roads in Ireland
had gone, that the big breakthrough came.

It is appropriate at this stage, not alone to describe the nature and type
of traffic on this turnpike road, but to quantify both the total traffic and
the various components of it and to attempt to estimate the tonnage of
merchandise carried. Before this is done, it is first necessary to describe the
positions of the various toll-gates.

Due to the absence of early records, the first information available on
the location of the toll-gates in county Dublin is from John Rocque's map
of 1762.[21] This map showed that the county Dublin gates were at Santry
(near the junction with Santry Avenue), at Lissenhall bridge about one

mile north of Swords and at Man-of-War inn approximately three miles south of Balbriggan. Matthew Wren's map of county Louth of 1766[22] showed that the toll gates in that county were at Killineer (north of Drogheda) and south of Dunleer village. Taylor and Skinner's *Maps of the roads of Ireland*[23] (1778) showed the location of all the toll-gates including the two others in county Meath at Gormanston and south of Drogheda. Thus there were a total of seven toll gates on the Dublin–Dunleer turnpike road. The toll-gate at Santry was changed to Drumcondra in January 1788[24] because it was being evaded at Santry. At subsequent dates new gates were added at Swords (south side) and at Julianstown county Meath while the one near the Man-of-War inn was later removed.

In the case of the Lissenhall toll-gate, it is fortunate that a complete set (some un-named but fitting exactly into the time sequence) of the toll books[25] for the year from 25 January 1818 to 24 January 1819 has survived. These toll books recorded for each day the units of traffic which paid tolls at the toll-gate together with the amount of the toll paid. Because these toll books are the nearest that can be obtained to a traffic count at that time, they have been used here to undertake a detailed analysis of the recorded traffic. It must be clearly understood of course that not all traffic which was on the road at that time was recorded in these books. The following classes of traffic were legally exempted: traffic which had already paid the toll that day either at the Lissenhall gate, or at other specified

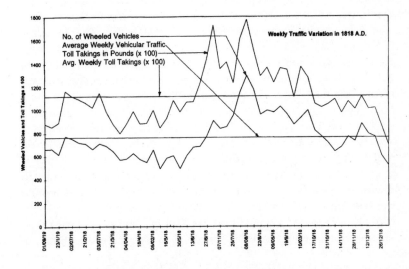

Figure 2 Weekly traffic variation at Lissenhall in 1818
(Source: Toll Books in F.C.C.)

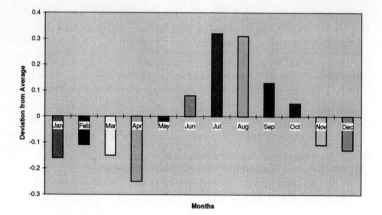

Figure 3 Variations in monthly toll-takings at Lissenhall in 1818
(Source: Toll books in F.C.C.)

gates; season ticket holders; military, or works vehicles and stage or mail coach services which paid quarterly at the head-office of the turnpike trust It is also possible that the gate-keeper may not have recorded all payments made to him or may have allowed vehicles of friends through the gate without payment, but after extensive checking, no evidence was found of any such wrongdoing. The surviving toll books were analysed to determine the average annual daily traffic (A.A.D.T.) of wheeled vehicles (see appendix); the weekly and monthly variation of the traffic throughout the year in terms of the appropriate averages, and the determination of which weekday had the highest, lowest and average traffic. The computed A.A.D.T. of wheeled vehicles in 1818 was found to be 110 and the average annual daily toll receipt was found to be £1 11s. 10d. While the A.A.D.T. is a measure of wheeled vehicles, the average annual daily toll receipts is a measure of the total daily traffic (wheeled vehicles and animals). The average annual daily toll receipts can therefore also be useful.

The weekly traffic, when plotted graphically against time in terms of wheeled vehicles and toll receipts showed a pattern which resembles the pattern of modern* traffic variation over a similar time-period, that is, below average at the start of the year rising to a peak in late July and early August and then falling towards the year's end with a small pre-Christmas rise (see Figure 2). The monthly variation also resembled the modern monthly variation on a similar road (see Figures 3 and 4). It is remarkable that the August traffic in 1818 was found to have been 1.31 times the

* The 1978 traffic factors as in reference 26 are still correct and in use at present (1996). Consequently they are referred to as modern or current.

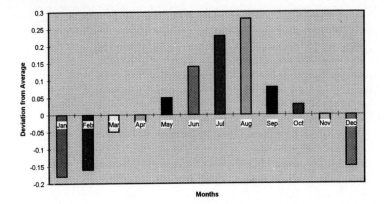

Figure 4 Modern monthly traffic variation on similar rural inter-urban main road (Source: John Devlin, RT 201 'Expansion factors for short-period traffic counts', An Foras Forbartha, Dublin 1978)

monthly average while the modern August (1978)[26] traffic is 1.28 times the monthly average.

The weekly analysis showed that the busiest day was Saturday, the slackest was Sunday while the average day was Thursday.

The composition of the traffic on the turnpike road at Lissenhall in 1818 was further investigated to ascertain the reason for the variation that was found in it. Three specific weeks were selected; the slackest week in the year (week ending on the second day of January 1819); the busiest week (week ending onthe eighth day of August 1818) and one of the average weeks (week ending on the seventh day of February 1818).

It was also decided to classify the total traffic into eleven distinct categories:

1 Coaches
2 Chaises
3 Gigs   Non-commercial traffic (categories 1 to 5)
4 Jaunting cars
5 Horses alone
6 Cars
7 Carts
8 Carts-and-cars*   Commercial traffic (categories 6 to 11)
9 Asses
10 Cattle
11 Sheep and pigs

The results of this analysis are shown in Tables 7, 8 and 9.

* This was a distinct type included in the toll books

Table 7 Composition of traffic at Lissenhall for week ending 2 Jan. 1819

Type of Traffic	Sun 27/12	Mon 28/12	Tues 29/12	Wed 30/12	Thurs 31/12	Fri 1/1	Sat 2/1	Weekly Total	Cat. % of Total
Coaches	0	0	0	1	0	0	1	2	0.31
Chaises	2	1	4	3	2	2	4	18	2.8
Gigs	6	1	0	2	2	4	0	15	2.34
Jaunting cars	4	1	1	0	1	0	2	9	1.4
Horses alone	10	22	9	10	17	21	13	102	15.89
Cars	4	12	27	13	14	6	17	93	14.49
Carts	6	10	22	31	52	39	34	194	30.22
Cars and carts	2	11	39	39	29	36	26	182	28.35
Asses	0	1	0	1	0	0	0	2	0.31
Cattle	4	0	0	3	2	0	0	9	1.4
Sheep and pigs	0	0	0	12	4	0	0	16	2.49
Total	38	59	102	115	123	108	97	642	100
Daily % of total	5.92	9.19	15.89	17.91	19.16	16.82	15.11	100	0

Table 8 Composition of traffic at Lissenhall for week ending 8 Aug. 1818

Type of Traffic	Sun 2/8	Mon 3/8	Tues 4/8	Wed 5/8	Thurs 6/8	Fri 7/8	Sat 8/8	Weekly Total	Cat. % of Total
Coaches	1	2	5	3	3	2	1	17	1.15
Chaises	2	10	3	9	3	6	6	39	2.64
Gigs	6	5	7	9	4	6	5	42	2.85
Jaunting cars	0	0	0	0	0	0	0	0	0
Horses alone	21	11	9	29	12	9	10	101	6.84
Cars	20	22	15	18	15	22	19	131	8.88
Carts	21	15	45	23	45	37	29	215	14.57
Cars and carts	73	118	159	150	178	150	36	864	58.53
Asses	1	2	0	1	0	0	1	5	0.34
Cattle	1	1	15	9	6	0	0	32	2.17
Sheep and pigs	0	0	15	15	0	0	0	30	2.03
Total	146	186	273	266	266	232	107	1476	100
Daily % of total	9.89	12.6	18.50	18.02	18.02	15.72	7.25	100	0

Table 9 Composition of traffic at Lissenhall for week ending 7 Feb. 1818

Type of Traffic	Sun 1/2	Mon 2/2	Tues 3/2	Wed 4/2	Thurs 5/2	Fri 6/2	Sat 7/2	Weekly Total	Cat. % of Total
Coaches	4	1	3	0	0	4	0	12	1.33
Chaises	3	2	1	5	3	10	3	27	3
Gigs	4	3	0	2	3	7	2	21	2.33
Jaunting cars	0	0	0	0	0	0	0	0	0
Horses alone	18	14	10	13	13	25	14	107	11.88
Cars	2	37	9	20	12	17	25	122	13.54
Carts	46	30	49	42	96	58	65	386	42.84
Cars and carts	7	7	64	54	5	56	8	201	22.31
Asses	1	0	1	0	0	1	1	4	0.44
Cattle	1	1	0	1	4	0	0	7	0.78
Sheep and pigs	0	0	0	10	4	0	0	14	1.55
Total	86	95	137	147	140	178	118	901	100
Daily % of total	9.54	10.54	15.21	16.32	15.54	19.75	13.1	100	0

The following general observations may be drawn from these tables: The August increase in traffic was largely due to the increase in carts-and-cars, that is, commercial traffic, which no doubt reflected the harvest work and hay deliveries to Dublin (the modern August traffic increase on such a road is largely due to holiday traffic). The numbers of cattle, sheep and pigs on the road were small at all times and there was an absence of wagons or heavy goods vehicles of any kind. The analysis shows that the position was the same in 1818 on this road as that observed by John Loveday in 1732[27] and by Arthur Young in 1776-9,[28] when they wrote of the absence of wagons or heavy goods vehicles.

A further analysis of the tolls paid showed that while the commercial traffic amounted to 81.75 per cent of the total numbers of traffic units, it amounted to only 69.6 per cent of the total toll receipts. The analysis also showed that a very minimal increase of one halfpenny on the wheeled commercial traffic, for example by raising the rate of cars from one and a half pence to two pence together with an increase of approximately twenty per cent on the wheeled non-commercial traffic would have raised the total toll receipts for the year 1818 from £3,996 15s. 1d. to £4,796 15s. 1d.[29] It can be seen from the previous chapter that such an increase would have been very welcome and enabled some of the outstanding debt on the road to be cleared.

It is unfortunate that the toll-keepers did not record in their books the nature or quantity of the loads being transported in the various commercial vehicles. However an approximate estimate of quantity can be arrived at by determining, as far as possible, the practical capacities of the vehicles. The three types of vehicles involved were the *cart*, the *car* and the *cart-and-car*. The *cart* was undoubtedly the Scotch cart. G.B. Thompson[30] quoted Ivor Herring[31] as placing the arrival of this cart in Ireland about 1800 and further stated: 'Linen carriers were again quick to realise the value of the Scotch cart as a vehicle with greatly increased carrying capacity.' Thompson then quoted Wakefield[32] about the value and use of this type of cart:

> The shafts, in consequence of the greater height of the wheels are more on a level with the part of the draught and by this constriction, a horse is enabled to draw at least 7 cwt more than a common car. These drays are used for bringing linen from northern Ireland to Dublin and are now [1812] universally employed in the agricultural labours of the country.

Cars: These were most likely the wheel-car which was used all over Ireland. It was both the farm vehicle and linen carrier and without its sides became the famed low-back car. The wheels were solid timber which were fixed to rotating axles. G.B. Thompson[33] said of this vehicle that it 'had received much support by linen-carriers who used it for taking linen to Dublin' asthey were capable of carrying over seven hundredweight.

Cart-and-Car: The entry for 'cart-and-car' in the toll books is, however, puzzling. The toll rates paid for these was between the rates for carts and the rates for cars. It is most probable that 'cart and car' was the toll keepers way of recording this unusual type of vehicle, which according to Thompson, was a hybrid from the Scotch cart and the wheel car, of which he stated:[34]

> From the former vehicle, it may have borrowed the free wheels on a fixed axle; from the latter, it certainly retained body dimensions and wheel size, which made loading and unloading a simple operation.

In order to estimate the total tonnage of goods transported on this road in 1818 the following practical capacities was assigned to the above three types of vehicles based on their description: Cart – fourteen cwt.; Cart-and-car – seven cwt. and Car – seven cwt. (Note twenty cwt = one ton). Using the average daily numbers of these vehicles (note: not the average of the three selected weeks) the estimated total tonnage transported in one year was about 14,500 tons.

FAIR TRADER COACH OFFICE,
NO. 5, CASTLE-STREET, BELFAST.

Mr. Heyn

has paid 8 - 6 for

an out-side seat, by Trader

to Newry on Sunday

the 22.d day of June 1828

35 lbs. Luggage allowed to any Inside Passenger.
25 lbs.   do.   do.   Outside Passenger.

A LIGHT POST COACH,
THE FAIR TRADER,

Starts from the above Office every Morning at Five o'Clock, passing through Lisburn, Hillsborough, Dromore, Banbridge, Loughbrickland, (stops at Newry for Breakfast,) Dundalk, Castlebellingham, Dunleer, Drogheda, Swords, performing the journey to the Coach Office,

Sackville-Street, Dublin,

In Thirteen Hours, after which it goes direct to

WALSH'S HOTEL,
NO. 5, BOLTON-STREET,

Where it discharges the remaining Luggage, and Passengers who may prefer that Establishment. The Coach starts from the adjoining

Office, No. 6,

Every Morning a Quarter Past Six o'Clock, calling for Passengers at the Office, Sackville-street, and proceeding on the same route, (Breakfast in Drogheda,) and arrives at the

Office, Belfast,

At Half-past Eight o'Clock each Evening.

Passengers are requested to send their Luggage before Eight o'Clock in the Evening, previous to their starting from the Offices, also to have each Parcel marked with their name.

Figure 5 Facsimile of old Dublin coach bill
(From Thomas McTear, 'Personal recollections of the beginning of the century',
in *Ulster Journal of Archaeology*, 2nd ser., v. (1899), p. 71

To complete the traffic picture on this road, it is seen from the *Treble Almanack* for 1818[35] that two mail coaches operated between Dublin and Belfast and one between Dublin and Londonderry. It is also seen that the two stage coaches operated between Dublin and Newry. All these mail and stage coaches operated in such a manner that a total of twelve coaches passed through the Lissenhall gate each day. This brought the minimum computed A.A.D.T. to 122 wheeled vehicles.

An allowance for the exempted vehicles, particularly those which had paid once at this toll-gate and which were not required to pay again if they returned within the same day must be added to the computed A.A.D.T. of 122 wheeled vehicles in order to get the actual A.A.D.T. It is difficult to assess what this allowance should be but my estimate is that it is at least fifty per cent of the computed A.A.D.T. thus making the actual or true A.A.D.T. at least 177 wheeled vehicles. (110 x 1.5 + 22)

It is fortunate that one visitor named Thomas Cromwell who travelled on the turnpike road in 1819 has left a written account of his journey[36] from Dublin to Swords:

> This part of our first journey to the north of Leinster, having been performed in one of the jaunting cars, we were subjected to the perpetual inconvenience of stopping to permit the passage of droves of cars of a somewhat different description (the agricultural) carrying hay and straw to the metropolis, these without the least compunction, struggling over the otherwise sufficiently wide road, in such a manner as to allow of no alternative but that of waiting until they had passed. The 'rule of the road' it would appear is in truth a 'paradox' to Irish drivers since on every direction post we noticed conspicuous instructions to them to keep to their proper side, notwithstanding which we were subjected every ten minutes to the delay complained of ...
>
> We observed several Scotch carts along with these agricultural cars ... whatever were the load, both car and cart, were uniformly drawn by a single horse.

Mr Cromwell's account of the traffic on the turnpike road in the Swords area at this time is in accordance with the findings of the detailed traffic analysis.

Another writer Mr A. Atkinson writing in 1813 of the nearby Dublin –Kilcullen turnpike road has left a good description of the traffic on the road,[37]

> ... so frequently thronged with carts, cars, carriages and foot passengers ...

[the traveller] will find several parts of the road, particularly if travelling in a gig or dog-cart, enough to employ him while whipping in to the way and out of the way, while steering clear of public coaches, of weak and disabled men, of apple women and tinkers and of a numerous tube of pedestrians.

This analysis of the 1818 toll book gives an account of traffic on the turnpike road and how it varied throughout the year. It provides a method by which any available traffic figures on other turnpike roads could be marshalled and compared. The analysis also demonstrates the long-term nature of the current expansion factors for short period traffic and provides a method of estimating the A.A.D.T. from any short-term counts available for this road in the first half of the nineteenth century.

As seen above it is possible to estimate with reasonable accuracy the A.A.D.T. for any suitable year, where a short-term current is available. It is fortunate that in December 1836 such a traffic count was taken by the directors of the Dublin and Drogheda railway company[38] in order to convince their shareholders of the advisability of proceeding with the construction of the proposed rail-link from Dublin to Drogheda. This privately taken count was carried out for the whole month of December 1836 and was taken on all roads between Dublin and Drogheda (see Table 10). One of the counting points was at Swords. From the full survey, counts showing vehicles only are shown in Table 10.

Table 10 Survey of Vehicular Traffic on main roads linking Dublin and Drogheda from 1 Dec 1836 to 1 Jan 1837

Counting point	Public carriages	Public gigs and jaunting car	Private 4 wheel carriages	Private gigs and jaunting cars	Merchandise cars or carts	Total of vehicles
1. Annesley bridge	25	4,428	1,298	4,498	10,008	20,257
2. Drumcondra	428	921	180	1,260	9,943	12,732
3. Glasnevin	1	437	255	1,074	4,463	6,230
4. Prospect	467	483	248	1,168	9,318	11,684
5. Swords	396	307	91	353	5,268	6,415
6. Duleek	475	240	198	224	2,069	3,206
7. Balbriggan	322	108	66	768	4,550	5,814

Source: *Report of the directors of the Dublin and Drogheda railway company to meeting of shareholders, 1 March 1839* (Dublin, 1839) app. No. 11, pp 15-18.

It is not strictly correct to compare results such as this with the 1818 figures, since the conditions under which the count was taken and the pre-
cise location of the counting point at Swords are not known. However
the figures from the count at Swords should bear some relationship to the
traffic figures at Lissenhall because both places are on the turnpike road
and only about one mile apart. The comparison made below is simply to
show how the 1818 analysis may be used.

Using the parameter established from the 1818 analysis – that the
December traffic is only eighty-nine per cent of the monthly average
(note the 1978 equivalent figure is eighty-five per cent) – the A.A.D.T.
for wheeled vehicles at Swords in 1836 is 232 which is higher than the
estimated 177 for Lissenhall in 1818. These figures indicate that either the
1818 estimate for unrecorded traffic was too low, or that traffic increased
in the intervening years due to the general population increase and the
greater desire for travel. The persons processing the 1836 traffic count for
the directors of the railway company prepared an abstract[39] setting out the
projected income from the rail-link based on the December count. In
order to arrive at the total yearly traffic they multiplied the December
totals by twelve, being obviously unaware of the fact that the December
total was only eighty-nine per cent of the monthly average. By so doing,
they underestimated the prospective income from the proposed rail-link.

The 1818 and 1836 traffic figures have provided evidence of the
amount and nature of the traffic which travelled on this road in the early
nineteenth century. In order to give a full account of travel on this road
especially in the early years, it is best to show the risks and hazards faced
by travellers and other road users. There is only space to give isolated
examples of such events on this turnpike road. In case of accidents one
particularly sad one was reported in the *Freeman's Journal* in 1789:[40]

> Last Monday, as the mail coach was going to Drogheda, a woman
> near the Man-of-War threw some dirty water out of a cabbin
> which affrighted the horses in such a manner that they ran over a
> boy of five years old and killed him on the spot.

Stoppages of traffic were also experienced as this extract from Walker's
Hibernian Magazine in 1802 shows:[41]

> The Belfast mail-coach coming to town was obliged to stop from
> five o'clock until nine upon the road between Turvey and Swords,
> where a river runs, so great was the deluge.

For the week ending on the seventh day of February 1831,[42] the tolls
received at the Drumcondra gate were a mere £1 12s. 8d., where the

Table 11 Numbers of rewards paid by the grand jury of County Louth for apprehension or killing of tories, rapparees or other offenders

Year	Number of Rewards
1713	1
1714	1
1715	1
1716	8
1717	3
1718	0
1719	9
1720	14
1721	1
1722	5
1723	6(7)
1724	1
1725	1
1726	7
1727	4
1728	2
1729	1(2)
1730	0
1731	0
1732	1
1733	0

Note: Numbers in brackets are rewards paid for offenders other than tories or rapparees

normal figure was approximately £10 per week. This was due to a great fall of snow.

However the biggest hazard to travellers on the Dublin–Dunleer turnpike road were highwaymen and robbers of various kinds. All parts of the road were affected between Dublin and Dunleer and such activities continued up until the 1820s. After the Cromwellian wars, some of the dispossessed Irish landowners and ex-soldiers viewed the robbery of the newly arrived planters as their only method of redressing the wrongs which they experienced. As time went on, the genuine rapparees were replaced by ordinary criminals called 'tories' or 'highwaymen' by the law. A. Marshall in his book *Irish Tories, Rapparees and Robbers*[43] stated: 'By the end of the first quarter of the eighteenth century all pretences to patriotism on the part of the outlaws had disappeared.' The Louth grand jury presentment book (1713-33)[44] gave details of rewards paid to individuals for the apprehension or killing of tories, rapparees and other offenders during that period. Details of the numbers of such rewards are listed by S.J. Connolly (Table 11).[45]

It appears that with the coming into operation of the turnpike road in 1732, the problem in county Louth was abating. However at the Dublin end of the road, crime was very much in evidence when, for example a report in the *Dublin Gazette* of October 1731 recorded that a linen carrier was robbed and murdered near Drumcondra.[46] It is not possible to list all such crimes but there were frequent attacks on stage and mail coaches over the years.

The Dublin–Dunleer turnpike road had its own particular highwayman, named Michael Collier or Collier the Robber (1780-1849),[47] who was born in Bellewstown, county Meath and 'terrorised' the area from the Man-of-War northward to 'The Cock' (another inn) at Gormanston. He mainly attacked mail and stage coaches as well as the carriages of the rich and so he achieved a type of Robin Hood status. But he was eventually captured and allegedly deported or else press-ganged into the army. At any rate, he returned years later to the area and died quietly.

Thomas McTear from Belfast writing in 1882[48] recalls travelling to Dublin some time before 1820 when the coach had to be escorted by armed soldiers between Newry and Drogheda, because of brigands who were reported to be stalking the roads. It can therefore be seen that travelling on the Dublin–Dunleer turnpike road for almost the first ninety years of its existence was at times hazardous.

Influences and Engineering

In the opening years of the eighteenth century Ireland was, in effect, ruled by a Protestant ascendancy. This ascendancy was dominated by about 5,000 individuals who had almost complete control of parliament, the grand juries and all public posts. Members of it owned practically all of the land on which the majority Catholic population lived as tenants. In the north of Ireland, the position was more complicated, in that the majority of the tenants were not Catholics but Presbyterians who had been brought in from Scotland. Generally the country was poor and famines occurred in the early eighteenth and nineteenth centuries. A major famine occurred in 1845-8 in which it was estimated that over one million people died and a great number emigrated. This is the context in which the operation of the turnpike roads must be viewed and assessed.

The population of Ireland increased steadily throughout the eighteenth century from a level of approximately 2.5 million[1] in 1700 to approximately 5.3 million[2] in 1800. After 1800 it increased more rapidly reaching a level of 8.2[3] million in 1841. The growth in trade during the eighteenth century can be seen from Table.1. These population and trade increases tended to increase the traffic on all roads including the Dublin-Dunleer turnpike road.

In the case of the traffic on this road the most important influences were the continuing increase in the population of Dublin and the fortunes of the linen trade. The population of Dublin increased from approximately 80,000 in 1731 to about 129,000 in 1771.[4] However the fortunes of the linen trade had the greatest effect on the traffic on this road over the next fifty or more years and so it is best to examine this trade in greater detail. In the early part of the eighteenth century, Dublin became the centre and chief port for the export for linen. The linen trade grew very steadily and rapidly through the century as table 12 below shows. (Note: This table was made up from figures taken from a larger table in *The Economic History of Ireland in the Eighteenth Century* by G. O'Brien[5] showing exports of linen cloth and from 1710 to 1779.)

As the bulk of the linen was produced in the north-eastern counties[6] of Ireland, the transport of linen formed a large part of the traffic on the Dublin–Dunleer turnpike road. However an act of 1759[7] initiated the abolition of the compulsory six-labour system and began a system of imposing taxes in order to raise funds for road works. This tax was viewed

Aspect approaching Drogheda

Aspect leaving Drogheda

Figure 6 Milestone at Julianstown, county Meath

Table 12 Exports of linen cloth from 1710-1770

Year ended 25 March	Yards of linen cloth exported
1710	1,688,574
1715	2,153,120
1720	2,437,984
1725	3,864,987
1730	4,136,263
1735	6,821,439
1740	6,627,771
1745	7,171,963
1750	11,200,460
1755	13,379,733
1760	13,375,456
1765	14,355,265
1770	20,560,754

as double taxation on the transport of their product by the linen producers of the north east, that is, they had to pay for the repair of the county roads to transport their linen to the turnpike road and then to pay the turnpike tolls in order to transport it to Dublin.

A decision was made to build a new large linen hall in Belfast which opened in 1785 and to export the linen from Belfast rather than Dublin. This prompted a change in the thinking of the Presbyterians of the north east of Ireland from the Belfast–Dublin axis to a Belfast–London one. The act of union in 1800,[8] which ended Dublin's status as a capital, further added to this change. The impact of this can best be seen from the figures for the export of plain linen cloth from the major Irish ports between 1771-2 and 1822-23[9]. These figures show that while the export of plain linen cloth trebled in those fifty-one years the amount exported from the port of Dublin did not increase at all. Consequently the number of vehicles transporting linen cloth from the north of Ireland on the Dublin-Dunleer turnpike road did not increase as it should have increased over that period. The other significant change in the linen industry was the emergence of Drogheda as a centre for the manufacturing of semi-bleached coarse linen between 1771-2 and 1822-3. This development helped to generate traffic on the county Louth and county Meath sections of the turnpike road.

A further industrial change which affected the Dublin-Dunleer turn-pike road was the growth of the town of Balbriggan. Prior to 1765 Balbriggan was only a small seaside village. In 1765[10] a local landlord built a very fine pier and harbour at this place. The landlord also reorganised the fishing industry and started importing coal. In 1780 a cotton mill was established in the then expanding town. The turnpike road originally by-passed Balbriggan and went from Balrothery via the Hill of Clonard to Gormanston. About 1770[11] a new bridge was built over the Delvin river north of Balbriggan and in 1773 Balbriggan was made a post town. Because of this, the section of the turnpike route from Balrothery to Gormanston was diverted so as to go through Balbriggan (see Map 3 for details of this change).

A matter which boosted the amount of traffic on all roads and espe-cially the main turnpike roads into Dublin was the 'corn bounty'. The 'corn bounty' was a subsidy or bounty paid by parliament on the inland carriage of corn from all parts of the country to Dublin. It was introduced in order to give Dublin an ample supply of flour and bread and indirectly to encourage tillage as against pasture in the country. The enabling act[12] came into operation in June 1758 and the rates of the bounty were as shown in the table below.

Table 13 Rates of bounty payable on inland carriage of corn from 1 June 1758

Commodity	Rate per mile
On 5 cwt. of flour	3*d.*
On 5 cwt. of malt	2½*d.*
On 5 cwt. of wheat	1½*d.*
On 5 cwt. of oats	1*d.*
On 5 cwt. of bere★	1½*d.*
On 5 cwt. of barley	1½*d.*

At first it was provided that the corn should have come from more than ten miles from Dublin but five miles was the distance fixed by an amend-ing act[13] of 1767. Arthur Young opposed this bounty. Among the reasons he gave for his opposition was that this bounty was only payable for corn which was transported by road and that this gave rise to a large unproduc-tive class of horse-drawn vehicles to 'tear up all the roads leading to Dublin'.[14] There is no doubt but that this bounty brought an increase of traffic to the Dublin-Dunleer turnpike road as well as to other roads.

It is regrettable that the bounties paid each year were not listed by road but by county. The following table 14 [taken from Arthur Young][15] shows the amount of bounties paid each year from 1762 to 1777 for the counties of Louth, Meath and Dublin.

★ Bere is a variety of barley

Table 14 Total corn bounty paid each year from 1762–77 for the counties of Louth, Meath and Dublin

Year	Amount in £
1762	506
1763	426
1764	396
1765	306
1766	269
1767	1,087*
1768	1,382
1769	2,742
1770	2,494
1771	1,667
1772	2,896
1773	3,074
1774	3,375
1775	3,226
1776	4,252
1777	5,323

This table shows that in sixteen years the amount of the bounty increased by a factor of ten for these three counties. The corn bounty continued to be increased and was later applied to transport by canals and river navigations as well as roads. The inland bounty achieved its purpose in ensuring that Dublin was well supplied with bread and in stimulating the changeover from pasture to tillage throughout the country. In 1784 another act[16] was passed by parliament which allowed bounties to be paid on exports of corn from any port in Ireland except Dublin and this led to a gradual diminution of the inland carriage or road bounties.

The long-term effect of the corn bounty system on roads was to make the carriage of goods by road more popular and more common. It also made many people familiar with the turnpike roads and so it may be regarded as a good influence as far as the turnpike roads were concerned. In 1788,[17] the solicitor general proposed a bill in the house of commons to deduct a sum of one halfpenny from every shilling paid as a corn bounty

* Note that the rise in 1767 was due to a 'once-off' payment of £620 in county Louth that year. The rise in 1768 may have been in some measure due to the ten mile provision in the 1767 act, though in other counties unaffected by this such as Wexford, the rise was even greater. The rise from 1768 onwards was most probably caused by the time-lapse in changing over from pasture to tillage.

in order to give a sum of £10,000 to the Dublin–Kilcullen turnpike trust
to improve the condition of that road. The solicitor general contended
that the 'corn cars were the principal cause of injury to the Kilcullen
road'. This however was unacceptable to other members of the parliament
who said that the corn cars paid their tolls and that if one turnpike road
received a subvention, all other turnpike roads would make similar claims.
The suggested subvention however showed that substantial numbers of
the corn cars were using the turnpike roads and that parliament was aware
that these roads needed another source of income apart from the tolls.
The payment of all inland carriage bounties ceased as a result of an act[18]
passed by parliament in 1797.

The development of other public roads including other turnpike roads
had a profound effect on the fortunes of the Dublin–Dunleer turnpike
road. The effect of these other roads was the introduction of an element
of choice, that is, whether an individual would pay to go from one place
to another by one route, when he could travel more cheaply or even free
of charge by another route? When faced by choices like this the prospective traveller often opts more on the perceived cost of the journey rather
than on the real cost. Thus he is immediately conscious of the toll-charges
on the turnpike road, whereas hidden costs like time-loss or effort to
ascend hills may not be so apparent. In cases such as this the turnpike road
would generally tend to be the loser.

The generally good condition of the public non-turnpike or 'county'
roads as praised by Arthur Young[19] and others, owes its origin to a series
of eighteenth-century acts. These included the act of 1727,[20] which specified that all roads were to be gravelled to a width of twelve feet and that
all new roads were to be at least thirty feet wide, and the act of 1739,[21]
which encouraged the building of new roads from 'market town to
market town'. Many new roads were also built under the post office acts[22]
at the start of the nineteenth century and later the Board of Works also
built roads in the south and west.

It is thus seen that the turnpike roads had to compete with a very
extensive network of roads. In the case of the Dublin–Dunleer turnpike
road it can be seen from Map 2 that this turnpike road is not the most
direct route between Dublin and Drogheda. In fact the most direct and
shortest road between these two places is a narrow road which runs
directly north through the villages of Knocksedan and Naul in north
county Dublin. Another good route from Dublin to Drogheda is via the
almost straight road to Ashbourne in county Meath. Thus there were in
effect three separate roads between Dublin and Drogheda, one to the east,
another to the west and a third midway between them. The eastern one
was the Dublin–Dunleer turnpike road. Later a small portion of the centre
one became a turnpike road from Dublin to Knocksedan but the remain-

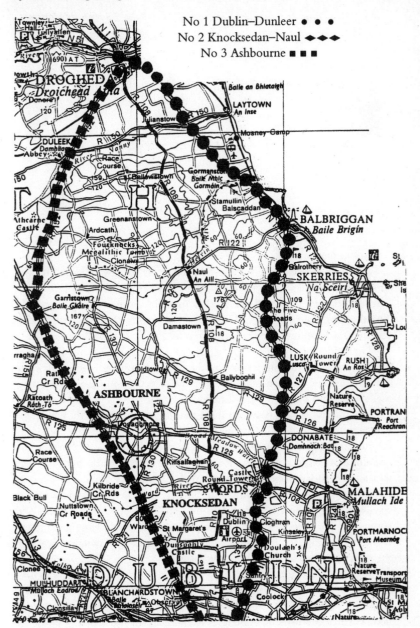

No 1 Dublin–Dunleer ● ● ●
No 2 Knocksedan–Naul ◆◆◆
No 3 Ashbourne ■ ■ ■

Map 2 Scale: 1 in 250,000.
Three roads to Drogheda. Based on the Ordnance Survey by
permission of the Government. Permit No. 6169.

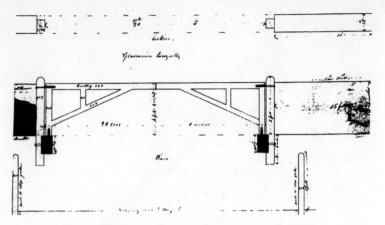

Figure 7 Drawing of a turnpike gate in north Dublin
(Source: F.C.C. Turnpike road records)

der of it was a narrow hilly road. Because of its narrow hilly nature, this
road was rarely used as a through-route between Dublin and Drogheda.
Later still the western road was made a turnpike all the way to Drogheda.
The distance from Dublin to Drogheda was twenty-three and a half Irish
miles by the Dublin–Dunleer turnpike road and by the Ashbourne road.

The effect of the opening up of the Dublin–Ashbourne–Drogheda
turnpike road on the toll receipts of the Dublin–Dunleer road is shown in
the table of toll receipts submitted to the select committee on turnpike
roads in Ireland 1831-32[23] (see Table 4).

The intense rivalry between these two turnpike roads is shown by the
evidence of Sir Josiah C. Coghill to the above select committee when he
claimed that the Dublin–Ashbourne–Drogheda turnpike authorities had
not alone originally misrepresented the length of that road,[24] but that 'they
had altered the milestones so as to make Drogheda appear to be only
twenty-two miles from Dublin' and this may have helped to induce more
travellers to use the road. It should be noted that after many complaints
about the condition of the road surfacing and drains on the Dublin–
Dunleer turnpike road the post office had by this time switched some of
their mail coaches to the Ashbourne turnpike.

The biggest difficulty caused by other turnpike roads to the Dublin–
Dunleer road was the concentration of such roads on the northern and
western sides of Dublin. The effect of this concentration was so great that
it was one of the principal official reasons given for the winding up of the
Dublin–Dunleer turnpike road and also of all the other turnpike roads in
north Dublin in 1855. There were nine turnpike roads in all, clustered in
a very small area on the north side of Dublin[25]. By contrast there were no
turnpike roads on the south side of Dublin, as the only arterial road locat-

ed there (leading to Wicklow and Wexford) was never converted to a turnpike. Because of this comparisons were made between the north and south sides of Dublin and a certain amount of resentment built up.

The opposition to the proliferation of turnpike roads on the north side of Dublin was brought up many times in the evidence to the select committee on turnpike roads in Ireland 1831-32. An example of this was the reply[26] of Mr James Huffington when asked why the people on the north side of Dublin complained of the turnpike system more than those who had to pay for road repairs on the south side. His reply was 'because they are not only subject to the turnpike system but also to the county and baronial applotment equal to the people on the south side'. This opposition was again echoed in a pamphlet issued in 1849[27] on behalf of 'The county and city of Dublin anti-toll committee' in which the author was complaining about a petition to preserve the turnpike roads which:

> ... is signed by the trustees of these lines [turnpikes] and by other easy gentlemen who wish to continue the *turnpike cordon aristocratique*, in order to preserve the privacy of their villa residences which occupy the district between Dublin, Malahide and Howth.

As stated earlier, one of the official reasons given for the winding up of the Dublin–Dunleer and other turnpike roads in the Dublin area in 1855 was this concentration of turnpike roads in the north side. Mr Abraham Hayward, one of the commissioners of the Dublin turnpike inquiry of 1854,[28] concluded:

> The chief objection to the turnpike system as it prevails in the vicinity of Dublin may be comprised under the following headings: its vexatiousness, inequality and consequent injustice; the irresponsibility of its administrators and its consequent liability to abuse; its expensiveness and comparative inefficiency as regards the condition of roads.

Mr Hayward added:

> The districts south or south east of the Liffey are (with a single exception) free from tolls; and a large body of evidence was adduced with the view of proving that the comparative decline of the northern districts in point of wealth and population in late years has been mainly, if not exclusively, owing to the turnpike system.

The early road acts, for example those of 1613[29] and 1727[30] allowed for the appointment of surveyors to supervise the six-day labour system. The

Dublin–Dunleer turnpike road enabling act of 1731[31] allowed the turnpike
trust to appoint its own surveyor at a salary of three shillings per working
day. The early surveyors on the Dublin–Dunleer road must have done a
reasonably good job on maintenance because there are no records of complaints. They were probably guided by recommendations or directives
issued by the Royal Dublin Society in 1736 and 1737[32] which were sur-
prisingly modern. The main recommendations were, the necessity of
laying good foundations, the use of gravel with provision of proper
camber and the necessity of laying the gravel in layers with the best gravel
on the surface. The Royal Dublin Society directions then stated:

> that gravel was at that time being used on the Irish turnpike roads
> and that, as a result, these turnpike roads were deemed to be the
> finest in Europe.[33]

However the work of making and repairing roads was becoming a sci-
entific instead of an amateur pursuit. In France, Pierre Trésaquet (b. 1716)
'was one of the first to introduce the idea that road building was suscepti-
ble to the operations of science'.[34] As a result of his efforts the French
main roads were in a very good condition in the last quarter of the eighteenth century. In Britain, two famous Scotsmen were to bring about
great changes in road building and maintenance. One of these was
Thomas Telford born in 1756 and the other was John Loudon McAdam
born in 1755. Telford who worked on roads, bridges and canals realised
that all these transport systems and structures were subject to the same
basic principles; they should be built on solid foundations; they should be
built properly and economically and in such a manner that they would
endure to fulfill their functions over a long period of years. Telford was
the founder of the Institution of Civil Engineers and its first president.
John Loudon McAdam was also an innovative road engineer whose sur-
name is now universally used to describe material consisting of broken
stone less than two inches in size.

In Ireland, one of the first of these new professional civil engineers
who worked on roads in south and west of Ireland was Richard Griffith
(later knighted) who is probably best remembered for the valuation of
Ireland for rating purposes (Griffith's valuation). The Irish grand juries
were enjoined by an act of 1817[35] to have their presentments and payments certified by qualified civil engineers or surveyors. These qualified
surveyors eventually became known as county surveyors and before
appointment they had to receive a certificate from a board of civil engineers set up for that purpose.

The turnpike roads, including the Dublin–Dunleer road, generally did
not however choose to employ these new qualified surveyors or civil

engineers. In consequence of this, they spent money needlessly and did not achieve the proper results. In fairness to the Dublin-Dunleer turnpike road trustees, they later engaged William Dargan, an Irish civil engineer who worked on the London-Holyhead road under Telford, to design a major improvement in 1831 but he remained only a short time. This was confirmed by Sir Josiah Coghill on 30 March 1831 when he stated in evidence to the Select committee on turnpike roads in Ireland 1831-2 that 'Mr Dargan was employed on the Dunleer road but threw it up nearly a twelve month ago'. Sir J. Coghill also indicated that when Mr Dargan left he was not replaced.[36] At the same inquiry Richard Griffiths complained of the lack of engineering supervision and the consequent waste of funds. He recommended the setting up of a board to manage all the turnpike roads, and that: 'the Board appoint one general superintendent of roads who shall be a civil engineer'.[37] The inquiry quoted the evidence of John Loudon McAdam before the committee of 1819:[38]

> ... that the first effectual repair of a bad road may be accomplished with little, if any, increase in expenditure, that its future repair will be attended with considerable saving although with increased employment of manual labour.

From the above, there is no doubt whatever, but that if the Dublin-Dunleer and the other turnpike roads had employed a civil engineer in the early 1820s, the condition of the road and its finances would have been in a far better state. It should be noted that since the last quarter of the eighteenth century, the trustees had farmed out both toll-collecting and maintenance. In the later years of the existence of the turnpike road, there was a reversion to direct labour for maintenance but by then it was too late. The system of road maintenance by direct labour was one where the road workers were hired on a daily basis by the trustees and these men carried out the road repairs under the instructions of the trustees' surveyors or engineer, thus eliminating any profit making by third parties.

The first recorded major improvement work on the turnpike road was carried out in 1794 on the steep incline leading in to the town of Drogheda from the south side. This work is best described by the following excerpt from *The traveller's guide through Ireland* published in Dublin in 1794.[39]

> Entering Drogheda from the south side, there is a very noble improvement in the road carrying on and nearly finished; the steep bank going down to the town, which was formerly very dangerous and difficult, has been cut away in the highest point and the hollow ground filled up with it.

The next major work carried out was the reconstruction, widening and realignment of Drumcondra bridge. This bridge over the Tolka River was narrow and skew to the general line of the turnpike road and had no footpaths. The widening of this bridge was foreshadowed in a report of 1787 by Thomas Sherard who suggested clearing the approaches to the bridge.[40] The work on the bridge was carried out in the period from 1816 to 1818 and was a very worthwhile improvement. Some of the funds for the work on this bridge were provided by the grand jury of county Dublin who could pay for work on roads catering for post office mail coaches by virtue of the post office acts.[41] A drawing showing the plan and estimate for the work has survived in the Fingal County Council records. It should be noted that the ford upstream of this bridge was retained after the widening work. Such fords were used in very hot weather by timber-wheeled traffic to swell the timbers and so reduce rattling noise when travelling.

The largest improvement to take place on this turnpike road was the major realignment scheme from Ballough to Balrothery. This scheme was four miles in length and by-passed the steep hill at the Man-of-War inn. This improvement scheme was authorised under the act in 1789.[42] The design drawing for the scheme was prepared under the direction of Mr William Dargan, the engineer mentioned earlier. This design drawing is among the Fingal County Council records and is dated April 1831.[43] The work of carrying out the road realignment was completed in 1834 which is forty-five years after it was authorised. It should be noted that this re-alignment scheme or diversion put the Man-of-War inn permanently out of business (see Map 3 for details of this diversion). William Dargan later achieved considerable fame as a builder of Irish railways including the building of the first one from Dublin to Kingstown and later the Dublin to Drogheda Railway.

Railways began to be developed in the opening quarter of the nineteenth century, at first mainly for use in quarries, timber yards and mines. The man who made the greatest contribution to the adaptation of the steam engine for tractive purposes was Richard Trevithick (1771-1833).[44] The first regular public railway was the Stockton and Darlington Railway which opened in September 1825. The biggest break-through in development of railways came after 1829 with the invention of The Rocket by Robert Stevenson and soon railways became very popular. The Irish were not slow to adopt this new form of transport. In his book on Irish railways, F. Mulligan stated that a plan to build 'rail roads between Dublin and the north, particularly Belfast and the intermediate towns, with branches'[45] was one of first such plans in Ireland. The plan was drawn up by the Leinster and Ulster rail company at its meeting of January 1825 but

Map 3 Showing portions of road diverted in eighteenth and ninteenth centuries. Based on the Ordnance Survey by permission of the Government. Permit No. 6169.

it never went beyond the planning stage. The first Irish railway was opened in 1834 between Dublin and Kingstown*.

In 1836 a commission[46] was appointed by parliament to report on the best way of bringing railway benefits to Ireland. This commission found that there was no great demand for a direct railway line from Dublin to Belfast, but that the demand was directed more inland towards Navan and Kells from Dublin and towards Armagh from Belfast. This commission however stated that these lines should be linked and that a branch could be run from Kells to serve Drogheda. However some of the recommendations of this commission were ignored and private demands took precedence. The Ulster railway line from Belfast to Armagh began in 1837 and the section to Lisburn opened in August 1839. The people of Drogheda called for a link to Dublin. There was much argument as to whether this line should follow a more inland route or the coastal route. The coastal route was finally approved and the line opened on the eighteenth day of March 1844. It was not until April 1855 after the completion of the massive viaduct over the Boyne that the trains could run directly between Dublin and Belfast. So it can be seen that for the last eleven years of its existence, the Dublin–Dunleer turnpike road had to compete with the Dublin–Drogheda railway line. However, the threat of eventually having to compete with a railway line from Dublin to Belfast was always present. The effect of this competition on the toll receipts of the turnpike road is shown in table 15[47] which is taken from the report of the Dublin turnpike inquiry of 1854. This table shows that between 1844 and 1853 income was almost halved. At the same inquiry the treasurer of the Dublin-Dunleer turnpike trust seemed to believe that the downturn in tolls was due in some way to the decline in potato cultivation following on the famine in Ireland (1845-8) when he stated in evidence[48] that 'if the potato cultivation were restored, there would be a prospect of increasing toll'.

However the end had come for all Irish turnpike roads in 1855 and 1856. This end was brought about by the advent of the railways. The effect of the railways on the winding up of turnpike roads is best described in the *Report of the commissioner for inquiring into the propriety of maintaining or abolishing the several turnpike trusts now existing in Ireland 1856*.[49] This report stated:

> The traffic of the road thus absorbed, there follows a decline of income, and with it ensue all the consequences naturally incident to such condition. The course is uniform throughout its progress as given by the witnesses on most of the lines: 1st – A rich and prosperous turnpike road; 2nd – The appearance of a railway; 3rd –

---

* Kingstown is now Dun Laoghaire

Table 15 Toll receipts of Dublin-Dunleer turnpike road 1844–53

Year	Tolls collected at gates			Tolls received for public conveyances			Total toll receipt		
	£	s.	d.	£	s.	d.	£	s.	d.
1844	1853	0	0	788	9	10	2641	9	10
1845	1936	0	0	469	4	9	2405	4	9
1846	1900	0	0	482	12	0	2382	12	0
1847	1506	13	4	422	10	0	1929	3	4
1848	1584	6	4	387	10	0	1971	16	4
1849	1364	10	0	125	2	0	1499	12	0
1850	1437	4	4	25	6	0	1462	10	4
1851	1423	0	0	46	13	0	1469	13	0
1852	1392	0	0	46	13	0	1438	13	0
1853	1380	0	0	45	12	0	1425	12	0

The absorption of the traffic; 4th – The decline of income; 5th – The road failling out of condition; 6th – The trustees getting tired, and abandoning to the officials; 7th – The officials swallowing up the funds; 8th – The county repairing in self-defence; 9th – The cess-payers becoming discontented at paying tolls on a road which they themselves are maintaining. And this is the stage at which, all the turnpike roads in Ireland with very few exceptions, have arrived.

In view of above, there is no doubt but that the public had become disillusioned with turnpike roads, and winding up was the only solution.

The winding up of the Dublin–Dunleer turnpike trust took place as a result of the passing of an act in 1855.[50] The relevant grand juries took over the maintenance of the sections on the roads in their areas from the trustees and the transition was without acrimony.

Conclusion

The Dublin-Dunleer turnpike road was never in a satisfactory financial position. To rectify matters the response from parliament or government was generally to raise the tolls, which was often only effective for a short period of time. The best period of the road from an income point of view, was 1790-1820 when the post office made payments for running mail-coaches on the road, and the general trade increase associated with the Napoleonic wars was at its height. Failure of the trustees to pay off its debts during this period was to have its consequences when trade decreased in the later years. Because of the great famine of 1845 to 1848 and the advent of the Dublin–Drogheda railway in 1844, the financial position deteriorated so badly that winding-up of the trust was the only practical solution.

An analysis has been presented of the use that was made of the road over the years giving a sample of the people who travelled on it and how they were facilitated in inns. A detailed analysis was made of the traffic in 1818 to show the amount and nature of this traffic and the number of vehicles of each type which used the road at different times of the year. A method was derived from this analysis which could be used in any further studies.

Finally some of the factors which influenced the progress and use of this turnpike road were investigated in detail. Many of these factors were completely external to the road, for example political developments in the northern part of the country and the coming of the railways. Other factors such as the failure to engage a qualified civil engineer or surveyor in a permanent capacity to supervise road maintenance from 1820 onwards were internal decisions.

These issues are only different facets of the total picture. If an event such as the opening of an alternative route caused a lessening of traffic on the road, the financial position deteriorated because of the diminution of the tolls. On the other hand an increase of traffic caused more wear and tear on the road surface or carriageway, and this, if not properly or economically repaired, caused a further loss of funds. The three themes are therefore different approaches to the spiral of inter-dependencies which besets any such transportation facility.

In conclusion, there was insufficient planning prior to the original decision to set up this turnpike trust or road and far too much was expected from the income of the tolls. The numbers of the trustees appointed to manage the operation of the road were far too great in the early stages. When it was obvious that the trust was in financial trouble, parliament or the government should have given a subsidy or grant to clear the debt. The laws continued to try to suit the traffic to the road, for example encouraging the use of broad wheels, instead of suiting the road to the traffic. Each particular turnpike road operated on its own as if the other turnpike trusts and roads even on the same long distance route, for example Dublin to Belfast, never existed. Finally it must be said that the Irish turnpike roads were a lost opportunity. If they had been combined into a national network as hinted at by Dr Cooper in 1758 or advocated by Richard Griffiths in 1832, they could have brought forward the concept of a national road network which did not emerge until the present century. Such a network would have ensured that the available funds were allocated to those portions of roads which were most in need and so brought about a uniform standard.

Appendix

TECHNICAL AND ARCHAIC TERMS USED IN THE TEXT

1 *Annual Average Daily Traffic* or A.A.D.T. This is a modern measure of the annual average daily number of wheeled vehicles using a road and is useful for comparing roads and for determining the form which a road should take, for example whether it should be a single or dual-carriageway or a motorway. It is simply calculated by adding together each day's traffic for the whole year and dividing by 365.

2 *Causey* This means a paved roadway or a raised road across marshy ground similar to a modern causeway.

3 *Condenser* When used in conjunction with a steam engine, a condenser is a separate vessel from the piston cylinder where the steam is condensed at a low temperature after leaving the cylinder at a high temperature. The invention of the condenser by James Watt greatly increased the efficiency of such engines.

4 *Streak, straike or strake* When used in connection with wheels, any one of these words means an iron band or shoe affixed to the rim of the timber wheel so as to strengthen it and prevent wear. These streaks or bands were affixed to wheels in former times with spikes driven into the timber rims. When these spikes or nails are driven in beyond the surface of the band or countersunk, the surface of the wheel is smooth. Sometimes the spikes were left protruding beyond the outer surface of the banding in order to give the wheels a better grip on steep grades or slopes. These were, however, much more damaging to the road surface than smooth wheels.

5 *Turnpike* The origin of this word is obscure. The explanation given in *The story of the king's highway* by Sidney and Beatrice Webb, is probably the most likely. In this book it is indicated that the word turnpike originated from the adoption in earlier times 'of horizontal tapering bands of iron or wood suspended upon a rigid vertical pillar, around which, as an axle, they revolved as a means of admitting outsiders to enclosed areas.'[1] Whatever the origins of the word turnpike, it became in practice a lockable gate or barrier, which could shut off access to a length of road unless a payment or toll was paid. The term *turnpike road* or even *turnpike* eventually came to mean a public toll road.

6 *Toghers* Embankments on peat bogs to enable roads to be carried over them.

7 *Place names* The locations of places are given in the text where possible and the towns and larger villages are shown on the various maps or drawings. There are however some places like the small but important village of Balrothery (located approximately one half a mile south of Balbriggan in north county Dublin), where the name was spelt differently at different times, for example Balruddery, Balrudd-erie or even Balrody. Great care is needed in such cases, though generally the sound of the name is often a better indication than the actual spelling. As much care as possible has been taken to avoid any confusion arising in respect of such names.

1 (London, 1913, repr.1963), p. 147.

Notes

ABBREVIATIONS

F.C.C.	Fingal County Council Archives
N.A.	National Archives, Dublin
N.L.I.	National Library of Ireland
T.C.D.	Trinity College Dublin
Q.U.B.	Queen's University Belfast
J.R.S.A.I.	*Journal of the Royal Society of Antiquaries of Ireland*
H.C.	House of Commons
Ir. Geog.	*Irish Geography* (Journal of the Geographical Society of Ireland)

GENERAL

1 *Dating*
Prior to the adoption of the Gregorian calendar in Britain and Ireland in 1752, the New Year began on 25 March. In addition, the adoption of the new style calendar involved advancing the date by eleven days. In this book, dating prior to September 1752, is according to the old style for the day and the month but according to the new style for the year.

2 *Measurement of Distance*
There is a difference between the statute, or English mile (1760 in yds) and the Irish mile (2240 in yds) which was used extensively in Ireland in the eighteenth and nineteenth centuries. The relationship between these measures is approximately 11 Irish miles = 14 statute miles. The following terms will be used here.
English or statute miles will be referred to as miles.
Irish miles will be referred to as Irish miles.

3 *Further Information*
Those requiring further details of traffic analysis at Lissenhall in 1818, of all changes in toll rates and of other matters should consult my original MA thesis (1995) headed 'A History of the Dublin Dunleer Turnpike Road 1731 to 1855' in the John Paul II library at St Patrick's College, Maynooth.

INTRODUCTION

1 Herbert Wood, *Guide to the records deposited in the Public Record Office of Ireland* (Dublin, 1919), p. 189.
2 E. O'Leary, 'Turnpike roads of Kildare, Queen's County, etc. in the eighteenth century' in *Journal of Kildare Archaeological Society*, vii (1912-4), pp. 118-24.
3 Joseph Lecky, 'The end of the road: the Kilcullen turnpike 1844-1848 compared with 1787-1792' in *J.R.S.A.I.*, cxiii (1983) pp. 106-20.
4 J.T. Fulton, *The evolution of the roads of county Down 1600-1900* (Unpublished Ph.D thesis, Q.U.B., 1972).
5 Sidney and Beatrice Webb, *The story of the king's highway* (London, 1913, repr. 1963).
6 *Journals of the house of commons of the kingdom of Ireland*, (15 vols Dublin, 1796-1800).
7 *Irish parliamentary registers, 1781-1800.*

ORIGIN, LEGISLATION AND FINANCE

1 J.P. Mahaffy (ed.), 'The early roads in Ireland' in *Hermathena*, xl-xli (1914-19), pp. 3-9.
2 John Woodhouse, *A guide for strangers in the kingdom of Ireland* (London, 1647).
3 Robert H. Murray (ed.), *Journal of John Stevens 1689-1691* (Oxford, 1912), pp. 108-9.
4 W.H. Patterson, 'A tour made in the north of Ireland by Dr Thomas Molyneux in August 1708' in *Proceedings of the Belfast Natural History and Philosophical Society* (1875) pp. 35-6.
5 Herman Moll, *A new map of Ireland* (London, 1714).
6 T. Gogarty (ed.), *Council book of the Corporation of Drogheda, 1649 to 1734* (Dundalk, 1988), pp. 350-63.
7 William Petty, *A geographical description of the kingdom of Ireland* (London, 1728), corr. and improved by John Bowles, map No. 4.
8 11-13 James I, c.7 (Irl.)
9 2 and 3 Philip and Mary, c.8 (Eng)
10 P. J. Meghen, *Roads in Ireland* (Dublin, 1965), p. 2.
11 10 Chas I, c.26 (Irl.).
12 L.M. Cullen, *An economic history of Ireland since 1660* (2nd ed. London, 1987), p. 54.
13 John Browne, *The benefits which arise to a trading people from navigable rivers* (Dublin, 1729), p. 4.
14 Jonathan Swift, quoted in Constantia Maxwell *Country and town in Ireland under the Georges* (London, 1940) revised ed. (Dundalk, 1949), p. 278.
15 *Journals of the house of commons of the kingdom of Ireland*, iii, 194.
16 Ibid., iii p. 613.
17 15 Chas II, *c.*1 (Eng.).
18 *Report of the commissioner for inquiring into the propriety of maintaining or abolishing the several turnpike trusts now existing in Ireland 1856*, p. xii, H.C. 1856 (2110), xix, 613.
19 3 Geo II, c.18 (Irl.).
20 *Journals of the house of commons of the kingdom of Ireland*, iv, p. 13.

21 Ibid., iv p. 15.
22 13 and 14, Geo III, c.30 (Irl.).
23 5 Geo II, c. 15 (Irl.).
24 7 Geo II, c. 18 (Irl.).
25 *Report of the commissioners appointed to inquire into the Dublin turnpike roads*, p. 63, H.C. 1854-55 (0.1), xix, 760.
26 Order for payment of interest on original debenture of the Dublin-Dunleer turnpike trust, 29 Sept. 1734 (N.A., M.5550).
27 *Journals of the house of commons of the kingdom of Ireland*, vi, p. 78
28 *Public Register or Freeman's Journal*, 1-4 Oct. 1763.
29 *Journals of the house of commons of the kingdom of Ireland*, vii, p. 283.
30 3 Geo III, c.30 (Irl.).
31 *Journals of the house of commons of the kingdom of Ireland*, vii, Part 1 app. clxiv.
32 13 and 14 Geo III, c. 28 (Irl.).
33 *Irish Parliamentary Register 1781-1797*, 1787, pp. 71-72.
34 27 Geo III, c. 59 (Irl.).
35 28 Geo III, c. 14 (Irl.).
36 29 Geo III, c. 23 (Irl.).
37 Records of Dublin-Dunleer turnpike road, F.C.C., Box 10, File 5.
38 *Report of select committee on the state of roads under turnpike trusts in Ireland 1832*, app. p. lvii, H.C.1831-2 (645), xvii, 691.
39 10 Geo IV, *c.*63 (U.K.)
40 *Report of select committee on the state of roads under turnpike trusts in Ireland 1832*, app p. lvi-lvii, H.C. 1831-2 (645), 690-691.
41 *Report of commissioners appointed to inquire into the Dublin turnpike roads 1854*, p. 17, H.C. 1854-55 (0.1), xix, 714.
42 18 and 19 Vict, c. 69 (U.K.).

TRAVELLERS AND TRAFFIC

1 Samuel Watson, *The Gentlemen's and Citizen's Almanack* (Dublin, 1733-1810).
2 *Dublin Journal*, 15-18 February 1746.
3 *Dublin Intelligence*, 1 May 1722.
4 Angelique Day (ed.), *Letters from Georgian Ireland, the correspondence of*

Mary Delaney 1731-68 (Belfast, 1990), p. 215.

5 W.R. and Lady Wilde, 'Memoir of Gabriel Beranger and his labours from 1760 to 1780', in *J.R.S.A.I.*, xiv (1876-78), pp. 138-41.

6 William T Wolfe Tone (ed.), *Life of Theobald Wolfe Tone* (Washington, 1826), p. 152.

7 John Gamble, *Sketches of Dublin and the north of Ireland* (London, 1811), p. 93.

8 *Leigh's new pocket road-book of Ireland* (3rd ed., London, 1835), p. 115.

9 J.F.T. Loveday (ed.), *Diary of a tour in 1732 through parts of England, Wales, Ireland and Scotland made by John Loveday of Caversham* (Edinburgh, 1890), p. 27.

10 Ibid, p. 59.

11 Constantia Maxwell, *County and town in Ireland under the Georges* (London, 1940, revised ed. Dundalk, 1949), p. 294.

12 Arthur Young, *A tour in Ireland in the years 1776, 1777 and 1778,* new edition, A.W. Hutton (ed.) (London, 1892, repr. Shannon, 1970), 2 vols.

13 Young, *Tour* i, pp. 105-8.

14 Young, *Tour*, ii, p. 77.

15 Young, *Tour*, ii, p. 79.

16 Young, *Tour*, ii, pp. 81-3.

17 Young, *Tour*, ii, p. 81.

18 *Dublin Journal*, 8-10 November, 1768.

19 *Cobbett's Evening Post*, 7 February 1820, quoted by Mark Searle in *Turnpikes and toll-bars* (2 vols London, 1930), ii, 733.

20 10 Geo IV, c. 43 (U.K.).

21 John Rocque, *Map of county Dublin* (1762).

22 Matthew Wren, *Map of county Louth* (1766).

23 G. Taylor and A. Skinner, *Maps of the roads of Ireland* (London and Dublin, 1778, 2nd ed. corrected 1783, repr. Shannon, 1969), pp. 1-2.

24 Records of the Dublin–Dunleer turnpike road, F.C.C.-TR/1 Minute book.

25 Ibid, Box 4, File 2.

26 John Devlin, *RT 201 – Expansion factors for short period traffic counts* (An Foras Forbartha, Dublin, 1978).

27 Loveday (ed.), *Diary of a tour 1732*, p. 59.

28 Young, *Tour*, ii, pp. 81-3.

29 *Report of select committee on state of roads under turnpike trusts in Ireland 1832,* app. p. xxix HC 1831-32 (645), xvii, 663.

30 G.B. Thompson, *Primitive land transport of Ulster* (Transport Handbook No 2) (Belfast, 1958), unpaginated.

31 Ivor Herring, 'The Scottish cart in Ireland and its contemporaries', *Ulster Journal of Archaeology,* 3rd series, i (1944), pp. 42-4, quoted in 30 above.

32 Edward Wakefield, *An account of Ireland statistical and political* (Dublin, 1812), p. 506, quoted in 30 above.

33 G.B. Thompson, *Primitive land transport of Ulster* (Belfast, 1958).

34 Ibid.

35 *The Treble Almanack,* 1818 (Dublin 1810 onwards). This *Almanack* replaced and incorporated *The Gentleman's and Citizen's Almanack.*

36 Thomas Cromwell, *Excursion through Ireland,* (2 vols London, 1820), i, 59.

37 A. Atkinson, *The Irish tourist* (Dublin, 1815), p. 216.

38 *Report of the directors of the 'Dublin and Drogheda railway company' to meeting of shareholders, 1 March 1839* (Dublin, 1839), app. No. 11, pp. 15-18,

39 Ibid.

40 *Freeman's Journal*, 18 June 1789.

41 *Walker's Hibernian Magazine*, 4 December 1808.

42 Records of the Dublin–Dunleer turnpike road, F.C.C. - Box 10, File 11.

43 A. Marshall, *Irish tories, rapparees and robbers* (Dungannon, 1927), p. 59.

44 Presentment book of the grand jury of county Louth 1713-33, N.L.I., MSS 11,949.

45 S.J. Connolly, *Religion, law and power* (Oxford, 1992), p. 205.

46 *Dublin Gazette*, 9-12 October 1731.

47 Enda O'Boyle, *A History of Duleek* (Duleek, 1989), pp. 58-61.

48 Thomas McTear, 'Personal recollections of the beginning of the century', *Ulster Journal of Archaeology*, 2nd ser, v (1899), p. 71.

INFLUENCES AND
ENGINEERING

1 K. H. Connell, *The population of Ireland, 1750-1845* (Oxford, 1950), p. 25.
2 Ibid., p. 25
3 Census of Ireland, 1841.
4 T.W. Moody, W.E. Vaughan (eds), *A new history of Ireland iv* (Oxford, 1986), p. 31.
5 George O'Brien, *The economic history of Ireland in the eighteenth century* (Dublin and London, 1918), p. 202.
6 Edith Mary Johnston, *Ireland in the eighteenth century* (Dublin, 1974), p. 93.
7 33 Geo II, c. 8 (Irl.).
8 40 Geo III, c. 38 (Irl.).
9 John Fitzgerald, 'The Drogheda textile industry' in *Journal of County Louth Archaeol. and Hist. Soc.* xx (1981), p. 48.
10 Arthur Young, *A Tour in Ireland 1776-1779* (London, 1780) 2 vols New edition. A. W. Hutton (ed.) (London, 1892, repr. Shannon, 1970) i, pp. 107-8.
11 P. O'Keefe and T. Simington, *Irish Stone Bridges* (Dublin, 1991), p. 145.
12 31 Geo II, c. 3.
13 7 Geo. III, c. 12.
14 Young, *Tour*, ii, p. 180.
15 Young, *Tour*, ii, pp. 167, 168.
16 23 and 24 Geo III, c. 19.
17 *Irish Parliamentary Register*, 1788, pp. 409-11.
18 37 Geo III, c. 24.
19 Young, *Tour*, pp. 76-81.
20 1 Geo II, c. 13 (Irl.).
21 13 Geo, II, c. 10 (Irl.).
22 32 Geo III, c. 30 and 45 Geo III, c. 43.
23 *Report of the select committee on the state of roads under turnpike trusts in Ireland 1832*, app. p. lvii H.C.1831-32 (645), xvii, 691.
24 Ibid., minutes of evidence. p. 85, 481.
25 J.H. Andrews, 'Road planning in Ireland before the railway age' in *Ir Geog*, v (1964), pp. 17-41.
26 *Report of the select committee on the state of roads under turnpike trusts in Ireland*, Minutes of evidence, p. 19, H.C. 1831-32 (645), vii, 415.
27 W.H. Hardinge, *Summary of authorities relating to the nine turnpike trusts on the north side of Dublin* (Dublin, 1849), p. 463.
28 *Report of the commissioners to inquire into the Dublin turnpike roads 1854*, p. 8 H.C. 1854-55 (0.1), xix.
29 11-13 James I, c. 7 (Irl.).
30 I Geo II, c. 13 (Irl.).
31 5 Geo II, c. 15 (Irl.).
32 'Directions for making roads', *Royal Dublin Society, Essays and Observations*, xxi, pp. 86-89 and xiii, pp. 89-93 (Dublin, 1736 and 1737) repr. London 1740).
33 Ibid.
34 Geoffrey Hindley, *A history of roads* (London, 1971), pp. 74-5.
35 57 Geo III, c. 7.
36 *Report of the select committee on the state of roads under turnpike trusts in Ireland, Minutes of evidence*, p. 80, H.C. 1831-32 (645), xvii, 476.
37 Ibid, pp. 151, 547.
38 Ibid., pp. 4, 400.
39 George Tyner, *The traveller's guide through Ireland* (Dublin, 1794), p. 2.
40 Records of Dublin–Dunleer road, F.C.C. Box 14, File 10.
41 32 Geo III, c. 30 (Irl.) and 45 Geo III, c. 45 (U.K.).
42 29 Geo III, c. 23 (Irl.).
43 Records of Dublin-Dunleer road F.C.C. maps No 4.
44 Philip S. Bagwell, *The transport revolution from 1770* (London, 1974), p. 90.
45 Fergus Mulligan, *One hundred and fifty years of Irish railways* (Belfast, 1952), p. 83.
46 *Second report of the commissioners appointed to consider and recommend a general system of railways for Ireland*, H.C. 1837-38 (145) XXXV.
47 *Report of the commissioners appointed to inquire into the Dublin turnpikes 1854*, p. 91, H.C. 1854-55 (01) xix, 788.
48 Ibid., pp. 64, 760.
49 *Report of the commissioner for inquiring into the propriety of maintaining or abolishing turnpike roads in Ireland 1856*, p. xviii, H.C. 1856 (2110), xix, 618.
50 18 and 19 Vict., c.69 (U.K.)